2nd edition

Oxford Discover Grammar

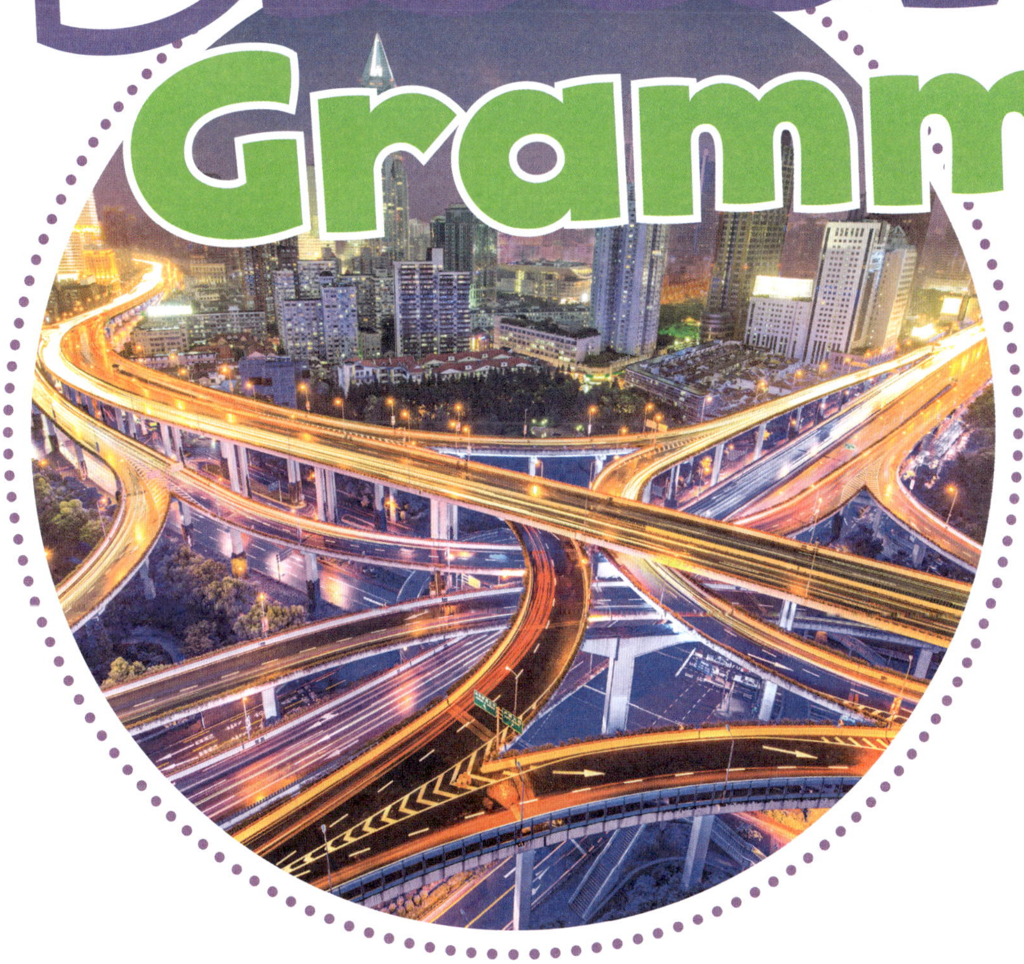

5

Angela Buckingham
Bryan Stephens

OXFORD
UNIVERSITY PRESS

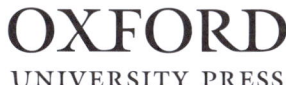

Great Clarendon Street, Oxford, OX2 6DP, United Kingdom

Oxford University Press is a department of the University of Oxford. It furthers the University's objective of excellence in research, scholarship, and education by publishing worldwide. Oxford is a registered trade mark of Oxford University Press in the UK and in certain other countries

© Oxford University Press 2018

The moral rights of the author have been asserted

First published in 2018

2024

11

No unauthorized photocopying

All rights reserved. No part of this publication may be reproduced, stored in a retrieval system, or transmitted, in any form or by any means, without the prior permission in writing of Oxford University Press, or as expressly permitted by law, by licence or under terms agreed with the appropriate reprographics rights organization. Enquiries concerning reproduction outside the scope of the above should be sent to the ELT Rights Department, Oxford University Press, at the address above

You must not circulate this work in any other form and you must impose this same condition on any acquirer

Links to third party websites are provided by Oxford in good faith and for information only. Oxford disclaims any responsibility for the materials contained in any third party website referenced in this work

ISBN: 978 0 19 405285 6

Printed in China

This book is printed on paper from certified and well-managed sources

ACKNOWLEDGEMENTS

Oxford Discover Photo Cover Credits: chuyu/123RF (Shanghai)

Oxford Discover Art Cover Credits: Sebastian Barriero

Illustrations by: **Galia Bernstein (NB Illustration)** pp.4, 6; **Fran Brylewska (Beehive Illustration)** pp.15, 37, 43; **Mark Duffin** p.66; **Andrew Elkerton (Sylvie Poggio Artists Agency)** pp.13, 14, 23, 26, 31, 40, 67, 71, 76, 77, 81, 89; **Martin Sanders (Beehive Illustration)** pp.19, 61; **Jorge Santillan (Beehive Illustration)** p.9.

We would like to thank the following for permission to reproduce photographs:
Alamy pp.5 (Heritage Image Partnership Ltd), 6 (Richard Levine), 8 (H. Mark Weidman Photography), 10 (Wavebreak Media ltd), 22 (Lorenzo Rossi), 27 (Oleksiy Maksymenko), 28 (bracelet/D. Hurst), 28 (coins/PjrStudio), 29 (bucket/Pick and Mix Images), 29 (tooth/Ryan M. Bolton), 30 (amphora/Carlos Mora), 30 (bone/Angie Sharp), 35 (Blend Images), 51 (David Pearson), 53 (map/travel images), 53 (whale/Wolfgang Polzer), 55 (polar bear/Stock Connection Blue), 55 (mountain/Photoshot Holdings Ltd), 55 (dog/RIA Novosti), 56 (Shakespeare/North Wind Picture Archives), 56 (Yuri Gagarin/Pictorial Press Ltd), 56 (Tchaikovsky/RIA Novosti), 62 (ruin/Peter Ekin-Wood), 62 (shops/David Bagnall), 63 (Eddie Linssen), 65 (garden/David Gee 3), 65 (past/Christine Osborne Pictures), 80 (plate spinning/imagebroker), 80 (tightrope/Ed Simons), 88 (parade/Hemis), 88 (flag/Laurent Davoust), Ardea pp.46 (Duncan Usher), 56 (kangaroo/Ferrero-Labat); **Corbis UK Ltd** p.60 (woman/Db2stock/Tetra Images); Fotolia pp.29 (vase/Alis Photo), 29 (coin/neftali), 29 (shoe/Kesu), 29 (fossil/smuki), 53 (wolf/rafi), 55 (dinosaurs/murphy81), 57 (Delphimages), 65 (field/tinadefortunata), 79 (JohanSwanepoel); **Getty Images** pp.7 (Frans Lemmens), 33 (Erik Simonsen), 55 (weatherman/Digital Vision.), 65 (now/Juergen Sack), 80 (tumbling/2011 Gamma-Rapho), 82 (WireImage), 85 (building/Cancan Chu), 85 (girl/Shannon Fagan); **Oxford University Press** pp.17 (girl/Blend Images), 28 (shoes/Photodisc), 28 (plane/Mark Mason), 29 (phone/Laurent Davoust), 44 (Amazon-Images); Rex Features pp.31 (Steve Meddle), 69 (Food and Drink); shutterstock pp.28 (ring/Elnur), 30 (crown/Ljupco Smokovski), 55 (vikings/Jef Thompson); **Superstock Ltd.** pp.11 (Felipe Caparrós/Age Fotostock), 19 (Biosphoto), 30 (hieroglyphics/ Science and Society), 42 (Biosphoto), 48 (NaturePL), 49 (age fotostock), 53 (family/ LEMOINE/BSIP), 53 (Olympic rings/ Xavier Cailhol/age fotostock), 53 (fireworks/ TAO Images/), 56 (Berlin Wall/ imagebroker.net), 58 (Stock Connection), 60 (volcano/ Tips Images); WWF International p.17 (logo)

Contents

 Finn  Sonya  Charlie  April

What Do You Know?		4
1 An Interview at a Zoo	Present Perfect • Present Perfect Continuous	13
2 Looking after Our World	Review of Tenses: Simple Present, Present Continuous, Simple Past, Present Perfect	17
Module 1 Review		21
3 What Can We Learn from Cave Paintings?	Modals of Ability: *Could / Couldn't, Will / Won't Be Able To*	22
4 A Presentation	Modals of Certainty: *Must, Has To, Might, Can't*	26
Module 2 Review		30
5 Our Future	Future with *Will / Won't* and *Going To*	31
6 A Spaceship Competition	Future with Present Continuous	35
Module 3 Review		39
7 Rescue!	Reported Speech with *Said That*	40
8 The Secret World of Ants	Reported Speech with *Told* and *Asked* • Reported Questions	44
Module 4 Review		48
9 Granny Stops Museum Thief!	Asking Questions • Subject / Object Questions	49
10 General Knowledge Quiz	Short Answers	53
Module 5 Review		57
11 Volcano	Passive: Simple Present Passive	58
12 A Changed Landscape	Passive: Simple Past Passive	62
Module 6 Review		66
13 A Rich Man's Fine Clothes	Adjectives and Adverbs	67
14 How Could We Make Our School "Green"?	Unreal Conditional	71
Module 7 Review		75
15 A Visit to a Science Museum	Sense Verb + Adjective	76
16 At the Circus	*It's* + Adjective + Infinitive	80
Module 8 Review		84
17 An Unusual Building	Articles: *A, An, The*, and No Article	85
18 The Castle	Review of Tenses: Simple Past, Past Continuous, Simple Present, Present Continuous, Present Perfect, Future with *Going To*, Future with *Will*	89
Module 9 Review		93
Exam Time		94
Grammar Reference		110

What Do You Know?

Predictions with Will

A Circle the correct words.

1 My brother **will / won't** watch the space program. He isn't interested in space.
2 They **will / won't** send more robots to Mars because they want more information.
3 I think we **will / won't** go on a trip to the space museum. Our teacher loves space!
4 We **will / won't** travel in space. It's too expensive.
5 I **will / won't** finish my space project. I don't have time.
6 My sister **will / won't** study space science at university. She wants to be an astronaut.

B Complete the conversation with *will* or *won't* and the words in parentheses.

Lucy   One day, tourists ¹ _____ (visit) the moon.
Kate   ² _____ (people, travel) there in space rockets?
Lucy   No, they won't. They ³ _____ (fly) in a space plane!
Kate   ⁴ _____ (it, be) dangerous?
Lucy   I'm sure it ⁵ _____ (not be) dangerous. I think everybody
          ⁶ _____ (have) a great time!

Future real conditional

C Circle the correct words.

1 If she **gets / will get** some money for her birthday, she **buys / she'll buy** a telescope.
2 **She'll look / She look** at the moon and the stars every night if she **has / will have** time.
3 She **won't / don't** see any stars if it **rains / will rain** tonight.
4 If she **visits / will visit** a space museum, **she'll learn / she learn** about the solar system.
5 If she **go / goes** to college to study space science, **she become / she'll become** an astronomer.

D Complete the sentences with the future conditional of the verbs in parentheses.

1 Scientists _____ (explore) new planets if they _____ (have) enough money.
2 If they _____ (find) water on these planets, it _____ (be) amazing.
3 If it _____ (be) too dangerous to land on a planet, they _____ (not go) there.
4 If they _____ (discover) a new planet, they _____ (give) it a cool name.
5 If they _____ (not build) a new spacecraft, they _____ (not land) on the moon again.

Verbs followed by Infinitives or Gerunds

A Complete the sentences with the infinitive form of the verbs in the box.

| visit   be   work   send   travel |

1 I want _____ an explorer one day.
2 I plan _____ around the world.
3 I need _____ hard at school.
4 I'd like _____ Peru.
5 I promise _____ you a postcard.

B Complete the sentences with the gerund form of the verbs in the box.

| read   look   come   watch   go |

1 My dad loves _____ films about archeology.
2 My mom prefers _____ history books.
3 I love _____ for information about exploring.
4 I really like _____ to museums.
5 My sister doesn't mind _____ either.

C Check the correct sentences. Cross out the wrong sentences.

1 My brother wants to be an archeologist.
2 He enjoys to learn about dinosaurs and things like that.
3 He began doing a project on dinosaurs at school.
4 There was a documentary on TV, but he forgot watching it.
5 My parents promised taking him to the Museum of Natural History.
6 One day, he'd like to discover some dinosaur bones.

D Complete the text with the gerund or infinitive form of the verbs in parentheses.

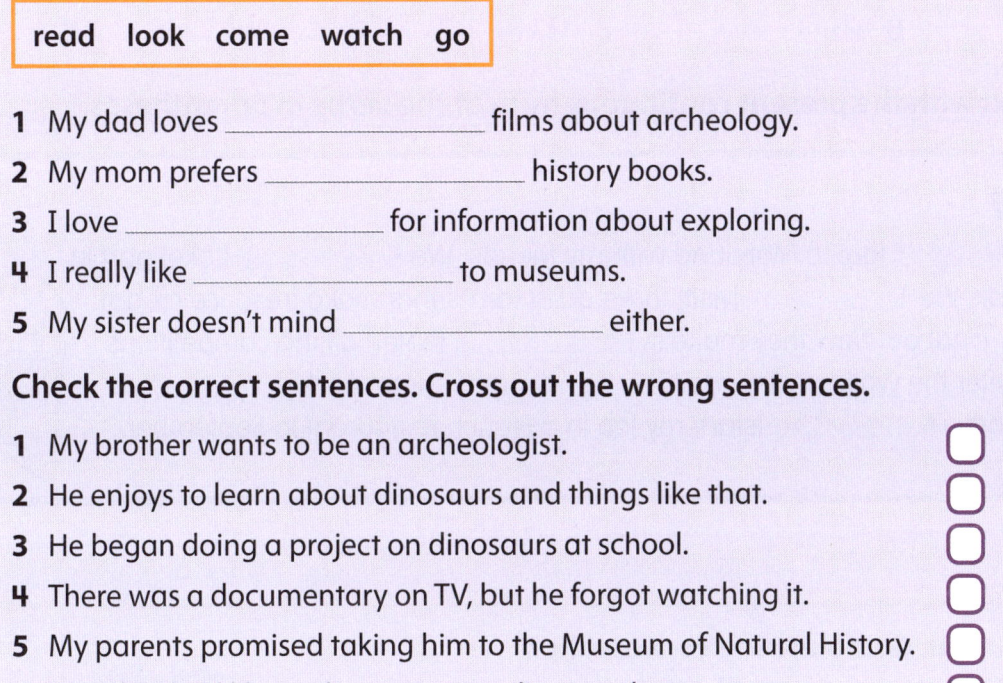

Hi Kate,

I'm having a great time in Mexico with my family, but we all want ¹ _____ (do) different things! My sister enjoys ² _____ (shop) and ³ _____ (eat) in restaurants. My parents want ⁴ _____ (go) sightseeing. I'd also like ⁵ _____ (visit) more ancient places. Yesterday, we agreed ⁶ _____ (drive) to Teotihuacan. It was amazing! There are mysterious and ancient pyramids there. I'd love ⁷ _____ (see) Palenque next, but that's a long way away.

Bye for now! Maria

Present Continuous for Future Plans

A Choose the correct words to complete the sentences. Write the correct letter (a–c).

My brother, Evan, wants to be a chef.
1. Next month, _____ a food course in London.
   a he takes   b he's taking   c take
2. Then, he's _____ to the U.S. with some friends.
   a travel   b traveling   c to travel
3. They _____ going to different food festivals there.
   a am   b is   c are
4. After that, Evan _____ starting a job in a New York restaurant.
   a am   b is   c are
5. I _____ him in the summer. I can't wait.
   a am visiting   b visit   c to visit

B Complete the text with the present continuous form of the verbs in parentheses.

Evan's blog

Tomorrow, I ¹_____ (go) to Maryland with my friends. We ²_____ (take) part in an ice cream walk. We ³_____ (visit) three dairy farms that make fresh ice cream. We ⁴_____ (find) out how they make it. I ⁵_____ (enter) all the competitions along the trail! After the walk, my friends ⁶_____ (go) home. And I ⁷_____ (travel) to New York. I ⁸_____ (start) my job in a French restaurant in September.

Polite Offers

C Billy is in a restaurant. Complete the conversation with the correct form of *would you like (to)*.

Waiter ¹_____ see the bill?
Billy   No, thank you. I'd like some dessert.
Waiter ²_____ some ice cream? It's our speciality. We have strawberry and pepper, chili-chocolate, banana and ketchup, …
Billy   Do you have vanilla?
Waiter Yes, we do. ³_____ have a topping? We have tomato and sugar, …
Billy   Do you have plain chocolate, please?
Waiter Yes, we do. ⁴_____ a drink as well? We have coffee and salt, …
Billy   No, thank you. Vanilla ice cream and chocolate topping is perfect.

6 What Do You Know?

Indefinite Pronouns with *Some-* and *Any-*

A Complete the sentences with the indefinite pronouns in the box.

> somewhere   anyone   anything   something   anywhere

1. I'm bored. I don't have _____ to do.
2. I don't have _____ to go.
3. Does Grandma have _____ to talk to?
4. Let's go _____ hot this year!
5. She'd like to do _____ artistic!

B Complete the conversation with indefinite pronouns.

Ben   Did you go ¹_____ good last weekend?

Luke   Yes! I went ²_____ really good – the beach!

Ben   Did you go with ³_____ else?

Luke   Yes, I went with my family.

Ben   And did you do ⁴_____ interesting there?

Luke   Yes! We did ⁵_____ very interesting! We took part in a sand sculpting competition.

Ben   Wow! Did you make ⁶_____ good?

Luke   Yes! I made ⁷_____ amazing. It was a sculpture of an elephant. My mom made a horse. My dad made a car, and my little sister made a bear.

Ben   Did ⁸_____ in your family win?

Luke   No! But it was great fun!

Offers with *Shall* and *Will*

C Complete the conversations with *shall*, or *'ll*.

1. Amy   I can't do my sand sculpture.
   Ben   _____ I help you?
   Amy   Yes, please.

2. Ben   I'm thirsty.
   Mom   I _____ buy you some lemonade.
   Ben   Thanks, Mom.

3. Dad   I'm hungry.
   Amy   I _____ get the sandwiches.
   Dad   Thanks, Amy.

4. Mom   Look at my horse sculpture!
   Dad   _____ I take a photo?
   Mom   Yes, please.

What Do You Know? 7

Indefinite Pronouns with *No-* and *Every-*

A Circle the correct words.

I live in a seaside town. In the summer, ¹ **everyone** / **everything** / **everywhere** wants to come here. But in the winter, there's ² **no one** / **nothing** / **nowhere** to do. ³ **Nothing** / **Everywhere** / **Everybody** is closed and ⁴ **nobody** / **nowhere** / **nothing** comes to visit. ⁵ **Everywhere** / **Everybody** / **Everything** stays at home. It's really boring!

B Complete the text with indefinite pronouns.

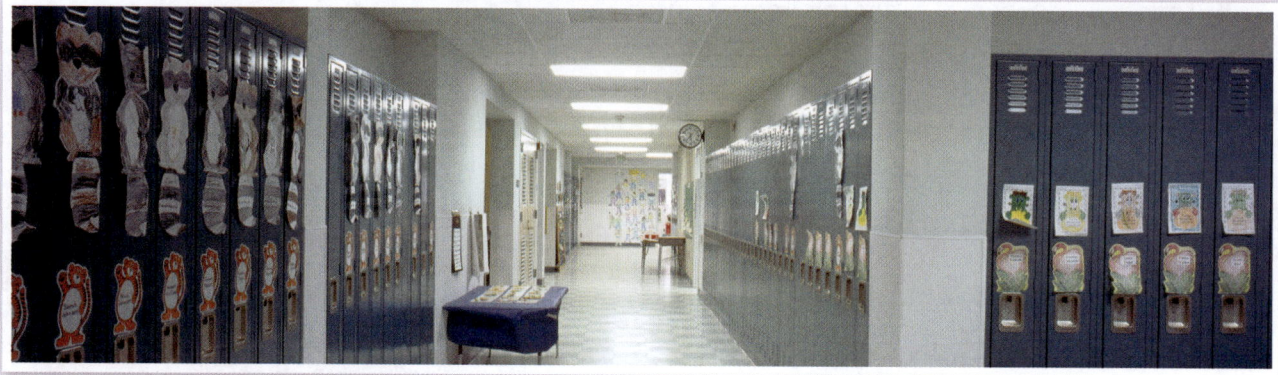

There are classrooms, but ¹ _____ is inside. There's a cafeteria, but ² _____ is eating there. There are corridors, but ³ _____ is walking there. I'm looking ⁴ _____ , but I can't find any people. Why is it so quiet? Why is it so empty? Oh! It's because it's the school vacation, and ⁵ _____ is at home!

Tag Questions

C Complete the conversations with tag questions.

1. Alice   You're from Tokyo, ¹ _____ ?
   Mai   Yes, I am.
   Alice   That's a very modern city, ² _____ ?
   Mai   Yes, it is.

2. Tom   Your dad has a new job, ³ _____ ?
   Sam   Yes, he does.
   Tom   You won't move to another town, ⁴ _____ ?
   Sam   No, we won't.

3. Olivia   You don't like fish, ⁵ _____ ?
   Ada   No, I don't.
   Olivia   But you will eat some meat, ⁶ _____ ?
   Ada   Yes, I will.

Order of Adjectives

A Check the correct sentences. Correct the wrong sentences.

1. Felix wants to be a doctor in a big, modern hospital. ☐
2. He wants to wear a nice, cotton, green coat. ☐
3. He loves doing interesting, new experiments at home. ☐
4. His parents bought him a huge, old microscope. ☐
5. He likes growing yellow, ugly mold in petri dishes. ☐

B Complete the sentences about children who entered a science competition. Use all the adjectives in parentheses, in the correct order.

1. Felix grew some _____ mold. (green / interesting)
2. Irene built a _____ robot. (tiny / fantastic / silver)
3. Sam created a _____ bag. You can use it again and again. (green / large / plastic)
4. Mara wrote a _____ idea about space. (new / fascinating)
5. Amy designed a _____ lab coat. It glows in the dark. (cotton / large / pink)

Used To

C Complete the conversation with *use to*, *didn't use to*, or *used to* and the verbs in parentheses.

Carlos Did you ¹ _____ (like) school?

Dad Yes, I did. I ² _____ (have) a great time with my friends.

Carlos Did you ³ _____ (enjoy) the lessons?

Dad Well, I ⁴ _____ (not like) history because I wasn't very good at it. But I ⁵ _____ (love) science. We ⁶ _____ (have) a brilliant science teacher.

Carlos What did you and your friends ⁷ _____ (learn) about?

Dad We ⁸ _____ (learn) about all kinds of things, like space and medicine. It was great!

What Do You Know? 9

Must / Mustn't and Have To / Don't Have To

A Choose the correct words to complete the sentences. Write the correct letter (*a–c*).

1. Magazines for young people _____ be fun.
   - a must
   - b have to
   - c don't have

2. Magazines _____ be on the Internet as well, but it's a good idea.
   - a mustn't
   - b don't have to
   - c have to

3. Editors _____ choose boring stories. The readers won't like them!
   - a don't have
   - b doesn't have
   - c mustn't

4. There _____ be interviews with famous people, but it helps.
   - a mustn't
   - b must
   - c don't have to

5. The photographers _____ take interesting pictures.
   - a must
   - b have
   - c don't have

6. Editors _____ print the magazine every week. It can be monthly.
   - a must
   - b don't have to
   - c mustn't

B Complete the sentences with *must*, *mustn't*, or *don't have to*.

1. Children's TV presenters _____ be confident.
2. They _____ look bored.
3. They _____ wear nice clothes, but it helps.
4. They _____ be funny, but children like it.
5. They _____ look at the camera and smile!

Present Perfect

C Complete the sentences with the present perfect form of the verbs in parentheses.

1. My dad _____ (become) a reporter on a local newspaper.
2. We _____ (start) a new school magazine.
3. I _____ (not do) my homework today.
4. A new sports center _____ (open) in our town.
5. My little brother _____ (not eat) his lunch.
6. My teacher _____ (give) us three tests this week.

D Complete Ella's news. Use the present perfect form of the verbs in parentheses.

I ¹_____ (do) lots of things this week. I ²_____ (be) to the new sports center. I ³_____ (swim) in the new swimming pool three times. I ⁴_____ (become) a reporter for our school magazine. I ⁵_____ (not write) a story, but I ⁶_____ (do) an interview. We ⁷_____ (work) hard at school. We ⁸_____ (not go) on a school trip yet. That's next week.

10 What Do You Know?

Present Perfect Questions and Short Answers

A Write the correct words to complete the questions.

1 Have you _____ first-aid before?
   a do   b did   c done
2 Have you _____ been outside in a storm?
   a never   b ever   c yet
3 Have you _____ someone in hospital before?
   a visited   b visit   c visiting
4 Have you heard about the earthquake _____?
   a just   b yet   c already
5 Have you seen the new hospital drama _____?
   a yet   b already   c just
6 Have you ever _____ to a paramedic?
   a speak   b spoke   c spoken

B Match the answers *a–f* to the questions in **A**.

a No, I haven't. I don't like TV programs like that.
b Yes, I have. I was in a park.
c No, I haven't. What happened? Is everyone ok?
d No, I haven't. I've never been in an ambulance.
e Yes, I have. I took a course at school. [1]
f Yes, I have. My grandmother was there for two days.

Present Perfect with *Already*, *Just*, and *Yet*

C Write the sentences and questions. Use the present perfect and the words in parentheses.

1 I / see / the news / today / . (already)
_____
2 the storm / start / ? (yet)
_____
3 the rain / begin / . (just)
_____
4 we / not hear / thunder / . (yet)
_____
5 my brother / lose / his umbrella / . (already)
_____
6 I / see / lightning / . (just)
_____

What Do You Know?

Present Perfect with *For* and *Since*

A Complete the sentences with *for* or *since*.

1 I've been interested in nature _____ a long time.
2 I've been a member of the school gardening club _____ last year.
3 I've wanted to work in forests _____ I was little.
4 I haven't been to the park _____ two days.
5 I've read books about trees _____ I was five.
6 I haven't been to the movies _____ the summer holidays.
7 I've been a member of the school football team _____ three years.
8 I've wanted to buy a new bike _____ months! Mine is too small.

B Write the sentences. Use the present perfect with *for* or *since*.

1 Lucy / live / in / California / six months / .
   _____

2 she / be / at her new school / January / .
   _____

3 she / make / lots of friends / she started / .
   _____

4 she / not email / her old friends / two days / .
   _____

5 her dad / work / in a forest / they arrived / .
   _____

Present Perfect and Simple Past

C Complete the email with the simple past or present perfect form of the verbs in parentheses.

Hi Lucy,

How's California? How long ¹_____ (you / be) there now? Well, I'm on vacation in Mexico at the moment. We ²_____ (arrive) on Saturday. It's amazing here. On Tuesday, we ³_____ (go) scuba diving. There are some amazing reefs in Mexico. I ⁴_____ (have) a lot of diving lessons before, so I can go and see them! ⁵_____ (you / see) any Giant Redwood trees yet? We ⁶_____ (study) them last month. They sound really interesting!

Write soon!

Alice

An Interview at a Zoo

Discover Grammar

A Listen and read. 02

Boy	Have you been working here for long, Mr. Abbot?
Zookeeper	Yes, I have. I've been working here for twenty years.
Girl	Have you done many different jobs at the zoo?
Zookeeper	Yes, I have. I've fed the animals, cleaned the cages, and I've spoken to children on school trips.
Boy	Have you visited the countries where the animals come from?
Zookeeper	No, I haven't. I haven't seen the animals in the wild.
Girl	Which animals have you been helping to protect over the years?
Zookeeper	We've been helping to protect lots of endangered species.
Boy	Have you been working with schools?
Zookeeper	No, we haven't, but we have been working with our interns. These teenagers have been helping us to improve our handouts for schools. Some have been doing jobs here on the weekends.
Girl	What sort of jobs?
Zookeeper	They've been brushing the ponies and feeding the animals.

B Circle the five past participles in the text above.

C Listen again and underline all the verbs ending in *-ing*. 02

D Reorder the words to make sentences.

1 animals / been / have / you / protecting / Which _____?
2 been / Have / schools / working / with / you _____?
3 been / here / doing / They've / jobs _____
4 ponies / brushing / been / the / They've _____
5 the / been / animals / They've / feeding _____
6 spoken / children / to / school / I've / on / trips _____
7 haven't / the / I / seen / wild / animals / the / in _____
8 interns / been / We've / working / our / with _____

Present Perfect • Present Perfect Continuous

An Interview at a Zoo **Unit 1** 13

Learn Grammar

A Read and learn.

Learn Grammar — Present Perfect

Use the present perfect to talk about things you've done in your life up to now (your experience).
Have you done many different jobs at the zoo?   I **have done** lots of different things!
Have you visited Africa or India?   No, I **haven't seen** the animals in the wild.

Affirmative: *has / have* + past participle
Negative: *hasn't / haven't* + past participle
Questions: *Have / Has* + subject + past participle *?*

Remember! The past participle is often the same as the simple past form of the verb.

TIP Some of the most common English verbs have irregular past participles, e.g. **eat → eaten, have → had, swim → swum**. There is a list on page 112.

Use short answers to questions in the present perfect to avoid repetition.
Have you fed the lions?   Yes, I **have**. / No, I **haven't**.

B Listen and read. Write sentences in the present perfect. 🔊 03

Sammy   ¹ _____ (you / do) lots of different jobs at the zoo over twenty years, haven't you?

Mr. Abbot Yes, I have. ² _____ (I / sell) tickets at the entrance, and ³ _____ (I / drive) the little train that goes around the zoo.

Sammy   Really? And have you done anything else?

Mr. Abbot Yes, ⁴ _____ (I / work) in the cafeteria, and ⁵ _____ (I / help) to build some of the things in the children's play area, too.

C Sammy has written an article about Mr Abbot. Fill in the blanks with the verbs below.

| he's driven | he's fed | He has been | he's helped |
| he's done | He's spoken | he's sold | He's worked (x2) |

An amazing zookeeper!

Mr. Abbot has been at the local zoo for over twenty years, and during that time, ¹ _____ many different jobs. ² _____ a lot with the animals of course, and ³ _____ and cleaned them, but he's also done lots of other jobs at the zoo. ⁴ _____ to school groups, ⁵ _____ tickets at the entrance, and ⁶ _____ the little train that goes around the zoo. But that's not all! ⁷ _____ in the cafeteria and ⁸ _____ build some swings and slides for the playground. ⁹ _____ a really amazing zookeeper!

14 Unit 1   An Interview at a Zoo

Present Perfect • Present Perfect Continuous

D Kadiatu works at the zoo on the weekends. Look at the pictures. Which jobs has she done? Which jobs hasn't she tried yet? Write sentences.

1. She's fed the penguins.
2. ___
3. ___
4. ___
5. ___
6. ___

feed the penguins ✓

work in the cafeteria ✗

sell balloons ✓

clean the picnic area ✗

help a lost child ✓

take some photos for the website ✓

E Read and learn.

Learn Grammar — Present Perfect Continuous

Use the present perfect continuous to talk about an action that started in the past and is continuing now. We often use it with *for* or *since*.
I have been working here for twenty years.

Past	Present	Future

Action started in the past.   Action is continuing now.

Which animals **have you been helping** to protect?
We**'ve been helping** to protect endangered species.
(= We are still protecting them now.)
Have you been working with animals a long time?
Yes, I have. / No, I haven't.

Affirmative: *has / have + been + -ing* form of verb
Negative: *hasn't / haven't + been + -ing* form of verb
Questions: *Have / Has + subject + been + -ing* form of verb ?

When we use the present perfect continuous in speaking, we often use the short form.
have = 've   I have been working. = I've been working.
has = 's   Mr. Abbot has been feeding the animals. = Mr. Abbot's been feeding the animals.

Use *for* to talk about a period of time, e.g. *five minutes, three weeks, two years*.
Use *since* to talk about a moment in the past, e.g. *ten o'clock, May 1, Sunday*.
I've been working at the zoo **for** three years.
I've been brushing the ponies **since** 7:00 p.m.

F Marta has written an email to her friend about the work she has been doing in the zoo. Read the email. Underline the seven examples of the present perfect continuous.

> Hi Laura,
>
> How are you? I'm great!
>
> I've been working for the past year as an intern at our local zoo. It's fantastic. I've been doing lots of interesting things. I've been working with lots of different animals in Pets Corner. My favorites are the meerkats. I've been feeding them. And I'm part of a group of interns – we have been preparing handouts for children who come to the zoo on a school trip. It's been good fun. What have you been doing this summer? Have you been working?
>
> I'll write again soon and send some photos. Bye for now.
>
> Marta

G Write the sentences in the present perfect continuous.

1. They _____ (do) jobs on the weekend.
2. They _____ (feed) the animals.
3. He _____ (speak) to children.
4. We _____ (not work) with schools.
5. We _____ (protect) the animals.
6. These children _____ (help) us.

H Make the sentences negative.

1. Yes, I've seen the animals in the wild. _____
2. Yes, they've been to Australia. _____
3. Yes, he's been telling visitors about the new animal. _____
4. Yes, she's been designing the new website. _____

Let's Talk!

I Tell your partner about some of the things you have or haven't done in your life. Take turns asking and answering questions. Use these ideas or your own.

> visit many countries   stay in my capital city   see animals in the wild   play soccer

Have you visited many countries?

I've / I haven't visited many countries in Europe and Asia.

J Take turns asking and answering questions. Use these ideas or your own.

> do my homework   play music in my room   draw pictures
> watch TV   do some exercise

What have you been doing today?

I've been playing soccer with my friends.

2 Looking After Our World

Discover Grammar

A Listen and read. Answer the questions. 🔊 04

My name's Selma. I'm a student at an international school in Turkey. I've been a member of the World Wide Fund for Nature (WWF) for years – since 2011. I joined because I liked the logo. Have you seen it? It's a picture of a panda, and I was crazy about pandas. But now I understand how important the WWF is, and I'm proud that I'm a member. The WWF started in 1961, and it has become one of the most important organizations in the world for conservation. Its members have raised money to protect animals' habitats, and they've held campaigns to protect the tigers. Right now they are working in Brazil to help protect the Amazon rainforest. Their work is continuing, all over the world. The other reason I like the WWF is because I know so many children around the world like me are members, too. It isn't just for grown-ups. We are doing something really important for our planet.

B Read again and answer the questions. Use the simple present, simple past or present perfect form of the verbs in parentheses.

1 When did the WWF start? It _____ (start).
2 What does it protect, animals or people? It _____ (protect).
3 How long has Selma been a member? She _____ (be).

C Look at the verbs in the text. Circle two examples of the present perfect. Highlight two examples of the present continuous. Underline two examples of the simple past.

D Circle the correct answers.

1 The WWF **started** / **has started** in 1961.
2 Selma **is** / **has been** a member since 2011.
3 Right now, the WWF **has worked** / **is working** in Brazil to protect the rainforest.
4 Selma **enjoys** / **enjoyed** being a member of the WWF.

Review of Tenses: Simple Present, Present Continuous, Simple Past, Present Perfect

Learn Grammar

A Read and learn.

Learn Grammar — Review of Tenses

Simple Present
Use the simple present to talk about facts and routines.

Affirmative: **Selma is** a member of the WWF. **She likes** animals.
Negative: **It isn't** just for grown-ups.
Questions: **Do** you **belong** to any organizations that help the planet?
Yes, I **do**. / No, I **don't**.

Present Continuous
Use the present continuous to talk about things that are happening now.

Affirmative: We **are writing** an article for our newspaper about the WWF.
Negative: **I'm not raising** money. **I'm helping** people find out about this organization.
Questions: **Are** they **trying** to help animals all over the world?
Yes, they **are**. / No, they **aren't**.

Simple Past
Use the simple past to talk about things that are finished.

Affirmative: I **joined** the WWF in 2011.
Negative: It **didn't have** a lot of members at the start.
Questions: **Did** your friends **join** as well?
Yes, they **did**. / No, they **didn't**.

B Circle the correct answers.

1. Selma joined in 2011. She is still a member. She **belongs** / **is belonging** to the WWF.
2. She is busy. She usually **writes** / **is writing** emails every month to tell the WWF about her wildlife campaign at school.
3. They always **visit** / **are visiting** their school garden.
4. Today, Selma and her friends are in the school garden. They **don't dig** / **aren't digging** the earth.
5. They **aren't drawing** / **don't draw** pictures at the moment. They are taking photos of the school garden.
6. They**'ve held** / **are holding** campaigns to protect the tigers.
7. Right now they **work** / **are working** to protect the rainforest.
8. Selma **doesn't think** / **isn't thinking** the WWF will publish her photos. But it does! She is very happy.

Review of Tenses: Simple Present, Present Continuous, Simple Past, Present Perfect

C Listen and read. Complete the sentences using the simple past. Then listen and check. 🔊 05

Q Where did bearded vultures live?
A In the past, bearded vultures
¹ _____ (live) in the Alps, which is a range of mountains in southern Europe.
Q Did they live in South America too?
A No, they ² _____ (not live) there.
Q When did they die out in the Alps?
A In 1913, humans ³ _____ (kill) the last bearded vulture in the Alps.
Q Did people kill the vultures by accident?
A Unfortunately, people ⁴ _____ (not kill) the birds by accident. People hunted the birds with guns and poison.

This is a bearded vulture. It's one of the species that the WWF has helped.

Q What did the WWF do to help?
A In 1978, the WWF ⁵ _____ (start) a project to raise the birds in zoos.
Q Was it easy?
A No, it ⁶ _____ (not be). It took a long time.
Q When did they release the first chicks?
A In 1986, they ⁷ _____ (release) some young birds in Austria, and then into some other countries, as well. They ⁸ _____ (not release) them into the Alps immediately.
Q Was the project successful?
A Yes, it ⁹ _____ (be)! Today there are more than 100 breeding pairs of bearded vultures in Europe.

The Alps

D Change the sentences into questions.

1 You sell copies of the school newspaper. Do you sell copies of the school newspaper?
2 It helps everyone learn about the WWF. _____
3 They learn about animals in the wild. _____
4 The WWF is working in many different countries. Is the WWF working in many different countries?
5 It is protecting animals all over the world. _____
6 Selma is writing a report for her school newspaper. _____
7 Arzur took some photos. Did Arzur take some photos?
8 Edul wrote an email. _____
9 They went to the school garden. _____

Review of Tenses: Simple Present, Present Continuous, Simple Past, Present Perfect

Looking After Our World Unit 2 19

E Read and learn.

Learn Grammar — Review of Tenses

Present Perfect

Use the present perfect:
- to talk about things that have happened up to now. These things happened at some time in the past. We don't say when they happened.
  The WWF has held campaigns to protect the tigers.
- to say that something happened in the past, but has an effect in the present. It is still happening now and is not finished or completed.
  It has raised money to protect animals.
- to say that something started in the past, but is still happening now.
  It has become one of the most important organizations for conservation.

Present Perfect or Simple Past?
The WWF started in 1961.
We know when this happened, so we use the simple past. Compare:
The WWF has worked in Brazil to protect the Amazon rainforest.
(The work is still happening.)
The WWF worked in Brazil to protect the Amazon rainforest. (The work is finished.)

F Write questions with the present perfect.

1. you / read / about the WWF? Have you read about the WWF?
2. your friends / work / in Brazil? _____
3. you / hold / a campaign for tigers? _____
4. she / write / for the school newspaper? _____
5. we / find / a photo of a panda? _____

G Circle the best answers.

1. They **saw** / **'ve seen** a vulture last week.
2. Have you asked Selma about the WWF?
   Yes, I did. / **Yes, I have.**
3. She **was** / **'s been** a member since 2011.
4. Julia **never went** / **has never been** to Brazil. She'd love to go.
5. I **fed** / **'ve fed** the tigers yesterday.

✏ Let's Write!

H Are you a member of a club, an association, an orchestra, or a choir? Write about it. Use these ideas or your own.

> be a member / Kids For Change / two years   join / 2013   proud / be a member

I've been a member of Kids For Change for two years. I joined in 2013. I'm proud to be a member. Kids For Change has done a lot of good work. It has raised money to help sick children.

> Review of Tenses: Simple Present, Present Continuous, Simple Past, Present Perfect

Module 1 Review

A Complete the email with the correct forms of the present perfect continuous.

Hi,

We ¹ 've been having (have) a great time here on our forest vacation. We ² _____ (go) on walks in the forest every day. We ³ _____ (watch) birds fly high in the trees. We ⁴ _____ (look) at lots of animals feeding or drinking near the river, too. Every morning, we ⁵ _____ (get up) early to see the sun rise. Then we ⁶ _____ (go) canoeing, and we ⁷ _____ (search) for pink dolphins! We ⁸ _____ (take) lots of photos, so I'll send you some in my next email.

Bye for now,
Jo

Hot Spot Why do you think tourists choose this sort of vacation? Is it the type of vacation you would like to go on? Why, or why not?

B Read and complete the text. Use the simple present, simple past or present perfect form of the verbs in parentheses.

Last week, our teacher ¹ _____ (ask) us to think of ways to promote World Car-Free Day at our school.

Cars are dangerous. They ² _____ (produce) dangerous gases that ³ _____ (make) people ill and cause pollution. They ⁴ _____ (be) noisy and they are very dangerous to children.

Last year, we ⁵ _____ (hold) a Walk-to-School week. It ⁶ _____ (be) a great idea, and lots of families ⁷ _____ (leave) their cars at home. Some children ⁸ _____ (walk) to school with their friends. Others biked. Some of my friends ⁹ _____ (make) a 'walking bus'. My friends ¹⁰ _____ (meet) me, and we ¹¹ _____ (go) together to the next house. The 'bus' got longer and longer. Twelve of us walked to school together that day!

I think World Car-Free Day ¹² _____ (be) really important!

C Circle the correct words.

1 Buses **cause** / **are causing** less pollution than cars.
2 Since the year 2000, Barcelona in Spain **closed** / **has closed** more than 300 roads to traffic.
3 A new tramline **has opened** / **opened** in Montpellier in France in the year 2000. Trams use electricity and are quiet, fast, and cheap.
4 In some English cities, children **have been walking** / **walked** to school on a Walking Bus, led by two grown-ups. This has been very successful.
5 Many countries **are building** / **build** more bike lanes, and there are bike rental programs in many cities.

3. What Can We Learn from Cave Paintings?

Discover Grammar

A Listen and read the information sheet. The fifth grade are visiting a Natural History Museum. 🔊 06

Frequently Asked Questions:

How could cave people keep their teeth clean if they didn't have toothpaste and toothbrushes?

They couldn't go to the dentist, but they could clean or pick food out of their teeth with sticks or bones.

Could cave people find food very easily?

They couldn't just go to the supermarket like us, but they could hunt, and they could also find fruit and berries in the forests. They also knew which plants you could eat and which ones you couldn't because they were poisonous.

In the future, will we be able to find out more about people who lived 20,000 years ago?

Yes, in the future, we will be able to know even more about these people, because of carbon dating and DNA.

Will we be able to learn more about what these people ate and how they communicated?

We will probably be able to find out what they ate, because of new scientific discoveries, but we probably won't be able to discover anything about the language they spoke.

B Find and circle the following words in the text above.

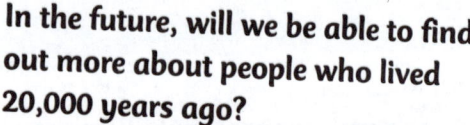

could   couldn't   will be able to   won't be able to

C Write 'P' next to the sentences that talk about the past. Write 'F' next to the sentences that talk about the future.

Modals of Ability:
Could / Couldn't, Will / Won't Be Able To

Learn Grammar

A Read and learn.

Learn Grammar — Modals of Ability

Could / Couldn't

I / you / he / she / it / we / they *could* + verb
I / you / he / she / it / we / they *could not* or *couldn't* + verb

Use the modal verb *could* / *could not* (*couldn't*) to talk about the ability to do things in the past.
Affirmative: **The cave people could hunt for food.   They could make fires.**
Negative: **She couldn't swim.   They couldn't use electricity.**
Questions: **Could they cook meat?   Yes, they could.**
             Could he go to the dentist?   No, he couldn't.

Will / Won't Be Able To

I / you / he / she / it / we / they *will be able to* + verb
I / you / he / she / it / we / they *will not* or *won't be able to* + verb

Use *will* / *won't be able to* to talk about the ability to do things in the future.
Affirmative: **In the future, we will be able to know more about cave people.**
Negative: **We won't be able to learn the language of the cave people.**
Questions: **Will he be able to learn more?   Yes, he will.   No, he won't.**

B Look at the picture and answer the questions with *Yes, they could* or *No, they couldn't*.

1 Could the cave men hunt animals with spears, and bows and arrows?
   _____

2 Could women and children hunt with the men?
   _____

3 Could the cave people cook their food?
   _____

4 Could the cave people keep warm by the fire?
   _____

5 Could wild animals get into their cave?
   _____

6 Could the cave people draw pictures?
   _____

C Listen and check your answers. 07

Modals of Ability:
Could / Couldn't, Will / Won't Be Able To

What Can We Learn from Cave Paintings?

D Circle things cave people *could* do in blue and things they *couldn't* do in red.

makenecklacesreadanewspaperusetoolsdriveacargotothesupermarketgotoschoolcookmeatmakeclotheslightafire

E Think of two more things that cave people *could* and *couldn't* do.

F Write two sentences with *could* and two with *couldn't*. Use the ideas above.

1 They couldn't go to school.
2 _____
3 _____
4 _____
5 _____

G Read the interview. Do you believe Mr. Jones? Find and circle the words *could* or *couldn't* in the text.

Interviewer	Mr. Batty, you say you have studied the cave people for a long time.
Mr. Jones	Yes, that's right. It has been interesting. I have learned a lot about their way of life.
Interviewer	Could they communicate with each other easily?
Mr. Jones	Yes, of course. They could speak perfect English, as well as their own language.
Interviewer	Really? That's amazing. And could they also write English?
Mr. Jones	Yes, but they couldn't spell very well, and they couldn't use a dictionary.
Interviewer	Could they live comfortably in their caves?
Mr. Jones	Yes, they could. Most of the caves had a bathroom and a kitchen, so they could take a bath or a shower, and they could cook food like we do. They didn't have refrigerators though, so they couldn't store meat for very long.
Interviewer	So you are telling us they had electricity?
Mr. Jones	Yes, they could light their caves like we do, but they couldn't install central heating.
Interviewer	Did you find any evidence of all of this?
Mr. Jones	No, I couldn't take any photos. I forgot to take my camera with me.

24 Unit 3 What Can We Learn from Cave Paintings?

Modals of Ability:
Could / Couldn't, Will / Won't Be Able To

H What do you think? Answer the questions.
1. Could the cave people communicate easily with each other? Yes, they could communicate easily with each other.
2. What languages could they speak? Yes, they could communicate
3. Could they also write English? _____
4. Could they spell and use a dictionary? _____
5. Could they take a bath or a shower? _____
6. Could they cook food like we do? _____
7. Could they store meat for very long? _____
8. Could they light their caves like we do? _____
9. Could they install central heating? _____
10. Why couldn't Mr. Jones take any photos? _____

I Match the two parts of the sentences.
1. Next year, I'll
2. He won't be
3. Could you
4. Cavemen

a. tell me more about cave people?
b. be able to study cave paintings at school.
c. could hunt with spears.
d. able to take photos without his camera.

J Write sentences with *could / couldn't* and *will / won't be able to*.
1. When I was six, / swim ✓ — When I was six, I could swim.
2. When I was four, / ride a bicycle ✗
3. When I was eight, / speak English ✗
4. When I am fifteen, / go into town by myself ✓
5. When I am 24, / travel around the world ✓
6. When I am very old, / run fast ✗

Let's Talk!

K Draw a picture of yourself when you were young. Show your partner. What could you do? What couldn't you do?

Imagine what you will be like when you are older. Draw another picture.

Ask your partner questions about their two pictures. Talk about your pictures. Use these ideas or your own.

- How old were you?
- Could you swim?
- Could you play the piano?
- How old are you in this picture?
- What will you be able to do?

Modals of Ability:
Could / Couldn't, Will / Won't Be Able To

What Can We Learn from Cave Paintings? Unit 3

4 A Presentation

Discover Grammar

A Listen and read the presentation for a school assembly. 🔊 08

Marco	Today we are talking about dinosaurs. They have found dinosaur bones near the school, so this part of the country must be where dinosaurs lived before.
Sara	Can you look at number 1 on the photo? The bone at the top of the photo must be the dinosaur's tail, and bone number 2 next to the tail has to be its backbone. We know this for sure because we can look at photos of bones found before.
Alex	And now, can you look at number 3 at the bottom of the photo? We know that the two large bones have to be the top of the dinosaur's legs. We think that bone number 4 near the man's tray might be the bottom part of the leg, but we are not completely sure. Are there any questions?
Student	Is that small object on the left of the photo one of the dinosaur's teeth?
Alex	No, it can't be one of its teeth. Look more closely. It's the man's hammer!

B Listen again. Then check (✓) *must*; circle *has / have to*; highlight *might*; and underline *can't* in the text. 🔊 08

C Read again. What do the presenters think is true and what do they know is true?

_____
_____
_____

26 Unit 4   A Presentation

Modals of Certainty: *Must, Has To, Might, Can't*

Learn Grammar

A Read and learn.

Learn Grammar — Modals of Certainty

Must / Has To
Use *must* or *has to* when you are sure that something is true.
The bone at the top of the photo must be the dinosaur's tail, and the bone next to the tail has to be its backbone. We know this for sure because we can look at photos of bones found before.

Might
Use *might* when you are not sure if something is true.
We think that the bone near the man's tray might be the bottom part of the leg, but we are not completely sure.

Can't
Use *can't* when you are sure that something is NOT true.
That can't be one of its teeth. It's the man's hammer!

B Read the sentences and complete with the words in the box.

> must   can't   might

1 This bone _____ be a leg. We are completely sure of that.
2 This bone _____ be a tooth. Maybe this is true, but we are not sure.
3 This bone _____ be part of the head. We are sure that it is not.

C Read the sentences and circle the correct words.

1 Everybody is 100 percent sure that this **must** / **might** be a dinosaur's tooth.
2 This **can't** / **might** be a dinosaur's egg because it's too small.
3 I am not completely sure that this is part of the tail. It **might** / **has to** be part of the neck.
4 The man working on this site **can't** / **must** be an expert because he has made so many mistakes.
5 We think that the bone near the tray **must** / **might** be part of the leg but we're not sure.

Modals of Certainty: *Must, Has To, Might, Can't*

D Reorder the words to make sentences.

1 at the top of the photo / The bone / the dinosaur's tail / must be

2 The bone / the tail / next to / its backbone / has to be

3 must be / the top of / the dinosaur's legs / The two large bones

4 on the left / The small object / can't be / one of the dinosaur's teeth

5 might be / near the man's tray / The bone / the bottom part of the leg

6 can't be / This / a dinosaur's egg

7 dinosaur's tooth / I am / must be / sure / this / a

8 be part of / has to / It / the neck

E Look at the objects. Match the two parts of the sentences.

1 I'm not sure, but I think this
2 I think this is made of gold, so
3 These are quite small, so
4 These round objects with an emperor's face
5 This object is made of plastic

a it might be quite valuable.
b must be Roman coins.
c so it can't be old.
d might be a toy.
e they must be children's shoes.

F Read and complete with *must*, *might*, or *can't*.

Rachel   What do you think this is? It looks like part of a toy to me.
James   It ¹_____ be because it's made out of gold. It ²_____ be something else.
         I think it ³_____ be a ring, but I'm not completely sure.
Rachel   Maybe you're right. And what about this broken pot? I'm sure that it ⁴_____ be very old.
James   No, it ⁵_____ be old. Look, it's made of plastic!
Rachel   And I'm not sure, but these round objects ⁶_____ be coins.
James   Yes, they ⁷_____ be. Look, there's a face and some writing on them.
         I think this ⁸_____ be Roman treasure.
Rachel   No, it ⁹_____ be. The Romans didn't come to this part of the country.

G Listen and check your answers.  09

✏️ Let's Write!

H Make sentences and say them to your partner.

> must   expensive   made of gold   might   child's shoe   quite small
> can't   Roman coin   made of plastic

> *I know it must be expensive because it's made of gold.*

I Imagine you have found some objects. Write a conversation like the one in **F**. Write what you think the objects *must*, *might*, or *can't* be. Give the reasons why each time. Use these ideas or your own.

Modals of Certainty: *Must, Has To, Might, Can't*

Module 2 Review

A Greg lived as a caveman for a week. Complete the interview with *could* or *couldn't*.

How was the week, Greg?

The cave was very cold, so I ¹_____ sleep at all. I ²_____ hunt small animals for food, but I ³_____ light a fire without matches, so I ⁴_____ cook them.

⁵_____ you find fruit and other things to eat?

Yes, I ⁶_____, but I ⁷_____ find any water to drink near the cave.

⁸_____ you spend another week in the cave, Greg?

Yes, I ⁹_____, but I don't want to!

B Read the interview and choose the correct words in the box. Write the correct letter (a–f).

> a we'll be able to do   b we won't be able to learn   c we'll be able to learn
> d We'll be able to travel   e we'll be able to answer   f we will be able to live

Interviewer Professor Bond, your new book is about the things ¹ __a__ in a hundred years. Can you give us a few examples?

Professor Bond Sure. Well, ² _____ many of the mysteries of history, for example, ³ _____ the language that the cave people spoke.

Interviewer No, ⁴ _____ how cave people communicated. That's impossible! OK, now can you tell us something about how ⁵ _____ differently in the future?

Professor Bond Sure. ⁶ _____ back and forward to Mars, for example.

Interviewer Interesting! Now let's ask everyone who's listening at home …

Hot Spot Do you agree with Professor Bond's ideas? Do you have your own ideas of what we will be able to do in a hundred years?

C Mustafa is an archeologist. Look at the photos of his discoveries. Write *must be*, *has to be*, *can't be*, or *might be*. Then match his notes to the photos.

1 It __must be__ Egyptian. I can see hieroglyphics!   __b__
2 It _____ a statue. It has two handles and a hole to put things in.   _____
3 It _____ valuable. It's made of gold!   _____
4 It _____ a dinosaur bone, but we aren't sure.   _____

5 Our Future

Discover Grammar

A Listen and read. A television presenter talks about the new invention he's going to present in next week's program. 🔊 10

In our next program, we are going to look at a new invention, the "Copterbike", which we believe will be a bestseller. Why?

It will work as a motorbike and will travel at 200 miles an hour! It will change to a helicopter in one minute and will fly at 400 miles an hour! You won't need to be a pilot to fly it, and you won't need to wear a helmet because there will be an airbag to protect your head. We predict the following with the "Copterbike":

- There will be fewer accidents.
- People will get to work quicker.
- Drivers will enjoy flying.

Good night, everybody. Next week, I am going to drive and fly the "Copterbike" myself, so I will be able to give you my opinion of the invention. Just have one last look at this beautiful machine. I think you can see that I'm going to have lots of fun! See you next week! Bye.

B Underline *will / won't* and circle *going to* in the text. What does the presenter use *will / won't* to talk about? What does he use *going to* to talk about?

C Listen and read the text again. Complete the sentences. Use *will*, *won't*, or a form of *going to*. 🔊 10

1 In our next program, we _____ look at a new invention, the "Copterbike".
2 It _____ work as a motorbike and a helicopter.
3 It _____ travel at 200 miles an hour.
4 You _____ need to be a pilot to fly it, and you _____ need to wear a helmet.
5 We believe there _____ be fewer accidents and that drivers _____ enjoy flying.
6 Next week, I _____ drive and fly the "Copterbike".

Future with *Will / Won't* and *Going To*   Our Future **Unit 5**

Learn Grammar

 A Read and learn.

Learn Grammar — Future with *Will / Won't* and *Going To*

Will / Won't

Use *will / won't* to talk about facts in the future.
The "Copterbike" **will** work as a motorbike and **will** travel at 200 miles an hour!
You **won't** need to be a pilot to fly it, and you **won't** need to wear a helmet.

Use *will / won't* to make predictions about things you believe.
There **will** be fewer accidents.
People **will** get to work quicker.
Drivers **will** enjoy flying.

Going To

Use *going to* to talk about future plans.
In our next program, we **are going to** look at a new invention.
Next week, I **am going to** drive and fly the "Copterbike" myself.

Use *going to* to make predictions about things you see.
I think you can see that I**'m going to** have lots of fun!

 B Read the TV presenter's diary for next week. What is he going to do each day? Write sentences.

Monday	Present the breakfast show
Tuesday	Interview the president
Wednesday	Present a children's program
Thursday	Work at home
Friday	Go to the dentist
Saturday	Fly to Paris on the "Copterbike"
Sunday	Not doing anything ☺

1 On Monday, he's going to present the breakfast show.
2 On Tuesday, _____.
3 On Wednesday, _____.
4 On Thursday, _____.
5 On Friday, _____.
6 On Saturday, _____.
7 On Sunday, _____.

C Listen to an interview with the TV presenter after the show. Write sentences with *going to*. Listen and check. 🔊 11

Interviewer you / drive and fly the "Copterbike" next week?
¹ <u>Are you going to drive and fly the "Copterbike" next week?</u>

TV presenter Yes, I / drive and fly it to the TV studios every day.
2 _____

Interviewer And / you / go on any longer trips during the week?
3 _____

TV presenter Yes, I / visit Paris on it on the weekend.
4 _____

Interviewer you / fly across the English Channel?
5 _____

TV presenter No, I / fly there.
6 _____

I / take the train under the English Channel.
7 _____

D Read the advertisement for a new weather satellite. Complete the sentences. Use *will / won't* and the verbs in the box.

| send ✓   provide ✗   circle ✓   have ✓   be ✓ |

Flash 1
Technical Information

Flash 1 ¹ _____ the Earth three times every day.

It ² _____ in an orbit 530 miles high.

It ³ _____ cameras to photograph cloud movements.

It ⁴ _____ TV images and telephone messages around the world.

It ⁵ _____ any information about the moon.

Future with *Will / Won't* and *Going To* Our Future Unit 5

E Read the conversation between two scientists about the weather. Complete the sentences with will or *going to*.

Scientist 1   Look at the dark clouds.
Scientist 2   Yes, it's ¹_____ rain in New York today. The picture is not very clear, though.
Scientist 1   Yes, I agree, but I hear the new satellite, Flash 1, ²_____ have much better cameras.
Scientist 2   Good. That ³_____ make our job easier in the future.
Scientist 1   Yes, it ⁴_____, but let's get back to work now! Look, the temperature in Colorado is minus five degrees centigrade.
Scientist 2   Yes, they ⁵_____ have a lot of snow today, especially on the mountains. But look here: there are clear blue skies over parts of the south.
Scientist 1   Yes, it's ⁶_____ be warm and sunny in Texas and Arizona.
Scientist 2   And look at the speed of the wind over Florida. There's ⁷_____ be a tornado there. Quick, call for help!

F Read the sentences and circle *will* or *going to*.

1. Next Monday, we **are going to** / **will** watch the science program about the "Copterbike".
2. Look at the satellite picture. I think it **will** / **'s going to** be hot and sunny later today.
3. Flash 1 **is going to** / **will** circle the Earth at a height of 530 miles at a speed of 4 miles per second.
4. I predict more people **are going to** / **will** use "Copterbikes" in the future.

Let's Talk!

G Write in the diary what you plan to do next week, then tell your partner your plans.

Monday	play tennis
Tuesday	
Wednesday	do aerobics
Thursday	go to drama club
Friday	
Saturday	watch soccer
Sunday	meet Sana

What are you going to do on Monday?

I'm going to play tennis with my friends. What are you going to do?

I'm going to go to drama club.

Unit 5   Our Future   Future with *Will* / *Won't* and *Going To*

6 A Spaceship Competition

Discover Grammar

A Listen and read the conversation. Look at the poster and the notes. 🔊 12

Awa	Next week after school, Sultan and I are meeting to design our model spaceship for the competition.
Mohamed	Jack and I are also planning our design next week, and we're hoping to finish the drawings on Friday.
Awa	We're finishing our drawings at the beginning of March and then we're making a test spaceship the following week.
Mohamed	So you're testing the spaceship to see if it flies in March?
Awa	Yes, and if everything goes well, we're building the real spaceship in June.
Mohamed	I think that's very late. The competition is in July!
Awa	So when are you building your spaceship?
Mohamed	We're starting to build it at the end of March and we're adding the solar panels at the beginning of April. We're planning to finish the whole spaceship by the middle of May. And we're testing it on June 1.
Awa	Wow!

Intergalactic Spaceship Competition!
Design and build a model spaceship
Final Entry Date Saturday July 24
First Prize $1,000

*Meet Sultan next week —
design spaceship
Finish drawings + make test model
(beginning of March)
Fly test spaceship (end of March)
Build final spaceship in June*

*Meet Jack next week —
finish drawings on Friday
Start building in March
Add solar panels in April
Finish spaceship in May
Test on June 1*

B Read the text again. Underline the verbs in the present continuous.

`Future with Present Continuous`

C Read the text again. Circle the correct answer, *a, b* or *c*.

The sentences in the present continuous tense talk about:
a plans in the present
b plans in the future
c plans in the past

D Write the base forms of the present continuous verbs underlined in the text in **A**.

1 _meet_
2 _____
3 _____
4 _____
5 _____
6 _____
7 _____
8 _____
9 _____
10 _____
11 _____
12 _____

E Act it out. Work in pairs and practice the conversation.

Learn Grammar

A Read and learn.

> **Learn Grammar — Future with Present Continuous**
>
> Use the present continuous to talk about future plans, especially when you mention a specific time or place.
> Next week after school, Sultan and I **are meeting** to design our model spaceship.
> We**'re building** the real model in June.
> When **are you building** the model spaceship?
> We**'re not building** it this year.
>
> **Remember!** Use *will* for future facts and predictions about things you believe.
> Use *going to* for future plans and predictions about things you see.
>
> Future fact
> **The prize for the spaceship competition will be $1,000.**
>
> Prediction about things you believe
> **I think that Mohamed will win the competition.**
>
> Future plan
> **I'm going to enter the competition next year.**
>
> Prediction about things you see
> **Look at the smoke from that spaceship! It's going to crash!**

36 Unit 6 A Spaceship Competition

Future with Present Continuous

B Listen and read. Complete the interview with present continuous affirmative statements and questions using the words in parentheses. 🔊 13

Intergalactic Spaceship Competition

List of finalists

1 Galaxy 1   2 Space Hopper   3 Big Bang 5   4 Blast Off 10   5 Enterprise 2

Interviewer	How many spaceships are in the competition?
Organizer	Here's the list. There are five finalists.
Interviewer	When ¹ _are you deciding_ (you / decide) who the winner is?
Organizer	² _____ (we / look) at all the designs on Monday and Tuesday next week. On Wednesday afternoon, ³ _____ (we / watch) the launch of *Galaxy 1* and *Space Hopper*.
Interviewer	⁴ _____ (the launch / happen) in Los Angeles?
Organizer	No, near Las Vegas. ⁵ _____ (we / travel) there on Sunday evening.
Interviewer	And when ⁶ _____ (other launches / happen)?
Organizer	⁷ _____ (they / fly) the other three spaceships next Friday morning at five o'clock.
Interviewer	And when ⁸ _____ (you / choose) the winner?
Organizer	⁹ _____ (we / meet) to discuss everything in two weeks.
Interviewer	Thanks very much for your time.

C Match the two parts of the sentences.

1 We're finishing
2 We're talking
3 The launches are happening
4 We're deciding
5 We're adding
6 We're flying

a the spaceship on June 1.
b the drawings on Friday.
c the solar panels in April.
d who the winner is in two weeks.
e about the designs next month.
f next Friday at five o'clock.

Future with Present Continuous   A Spaceship Competition   **Unit 6**   **37**

D Write questions for the sentences in **C**.

1 When are you finishing the drawings?
2 _____
3 _____
4 _____
5 _____
6 _____

E Circle the best option in each sentence.

1 Plan: Tomorrow at ten, we **are meeting** / **will meet** to discuss the competition.
2 Fact: The launch of *Galaxy 1* and *Space Hopper* **will be** / **is being** on Tuesday August 20.
3 Prediction (things you believe): Soon everybody in the world **will** / **is going to** have a cell phone.
4 Plan: They **are going to** / **will** launch the spaceship at this airport.
5 Prediction (things you can see): Look at that smoke! The spaceship **will** / **is going to** crash.

Let's Write!

F Work in pairs. Answer the questions with the present continuous, *will*, and *going to*. Write about yourself.

1 What are you doing tonight?
   I _____
2 How old will you be on your next birthday?
   I _____
3 What are you going to do during the holidays?
   I _____

G Take turns asking and answering the questions.

> I'm doing my homework, and then I'm meeting my friends.

H Write a letter to a new pen pal. Tell him or her about yourself. Tell your friend what you are doing next week. Use these ideas or your own.

- play sports on Tuesday
- watch a movie after school on Friday
- go out with friends on the weekend
- visit my grandma on Sunday afternoon

Unit 6 A Spaceship Competition

Future with Present Continuous

Module 3 Review

A Read the information for parents about next year's new school uniform. Write sentences with *will* or *won't*.

1 girls' skirts: blue ✓ black ✓ brown ✗
   The girls' skirts will be blue or black. They won't be brown.

2 boys' pants: long ✓ short ✗
   _____

3 boys' and girls' blazers: blue ✓ black ✓ red ✗
   _____

4 boys' and girls' sweaters: gray ✓ pink ✗ red ✗
   _____

B Match the two parts. Then write predictions with *I think* and *will*, or *going to*.

1 Those clouds look very dark.   a more at home.
2 robots / help   b much cheaper in ten years.
3 The bus hasn't arrived yet.   c We / be late for school.
4 space tourism / become   d It / rain soon.

1 Those clouds look very dark. It _____
2 I think _____
3 _____
4 _____

C Read the conversation. Complete the text. Use *going to* with the verbs in parentheses.

Anna   What ¹_____ (you / teach) the fourth grade next week?
Rachel In science, ²_____ (I / tell) them about some new inventions. In history, ³_____ (we / look) at inventions in the 1800s.
Anna   ⁴_____ (they / watch) a DVD?
Rachel Yes, ⁵_____ (I / show) them a DVD about the "Copterbike."
Anna   Great! And what ⁶_____ (they / do) in art?
Rachel ⁷_____ (They / make) some models.

D Look at James's notes. Write about his plans for next week. Use the present continuous.

meet Tony – Tuesday evening
go to park – Wednesday after school
see grandpa – Friday 5 o'clock

1 He's _____
2 _____
3 _____

Module 3 Review 39

7 Rescue!

Discover Grammar

A Listen and read the telephone call about a mountain rescue. 🔊 14

1	Ian	Hi Marc. We're looking for a German tourist. He called us from his cell phone. He was rock climbing and fell about 40 feet into a cave. He said that he couldn't get up. It sounds like a broken ankle.
	Marc	Does he speak English?
2	Ian	Yes, he does. His name's Felix. He has two friends with him. He said that they were getting cold.
3	Marc	Where are they?
	Ian	He said that they were near a lake.
	Marc	OK, I'm on my way.

Later that evening, on the radio…

4	Newscaster	24-year-old Felix Fischer broke his ankle when he was rock climbing today. Mountain rescue volunteer Marc Barclay said that the rescue went well. Felix is now in the hospital. He said that his leg wasn't very painful, and he thanked everyone for their help.

B Match the pictures to the numbers in the text.

C Look at the speech bubble text. How is it written in the text?

1 "I can't get up!"   He said that he couldn't get up.
2 "We are near a lake."   He said that they _____.
3 "My leg isn't very painful."   He said that his leg _____.
4 "We are getting cold."   He said that they _____.

40 Unit 7 Rescue!   Reported Speech with *Said That*

Learn Grammar

A Read and learn.

Learn Grammar — Reported Speech with *Said That*

Use **reported speech** to tell someone what another person said.
You can say what someone else said, or report what you said.

"Help! I'm stuck!" → She said that she was stuck.
"I can't read the map." → I said that I couldn't read the map.

To make reported speech, you usually change the tense of the verb from the present to the past.

simple present → simple past
present continuous → past continuous
present modal → past modal

Direct speech	Reported speech
I **am** in a cave.	He said that he **was** in a cave.
We **are getting** cold.	They said that they **were getting** cold.
I **can't** walk.	He said he **couldn't** walk.

You usually change the pronoun and possessive adjective, too.

Direct speech	Reported speech
I need some help!	He said that **he** needed some help.
We are lost.	They said that **they** were lost.
My leg is painful.	He said that **his** leg was painful.
Thank you for **your** help.	He thanked us (/ He said "thank you") for **our** help.

When you write in direct speech, use quotation marks to show that someone is talking.
"I'm on vacation," said Felix.

Don't use quotation marks in reported speech.
He said that he was on vacation.

B Look at the pictures and story on page 34 again. Circle the correct answer.

1. Who said, "I can't get up?" — Felix / Ian / Marc
2. Who couldn't get up? — Felix / Ian / Marc
3. Who said that he was looking for a tourist? — Felix / Ian / Marc
4. Who said that he was on his way? — Felix / Ian / Marc
5. Who was near a lake? — Felix / Ian / Marc
6. Who said, "My leg isn't very painful"? — Felix / Ian / Marc

Reported Speech with *Said That*

C Listen and read. Then circle the correct words. 🔊 15

"This is Bonnie. She's my mountain rescue dog. She helps me search for climbers who are lost or injured. Her sense of smell is incredible. It's 44 times more effective than a human's. Rescue dogs can rescue people in caves, mountains, and in areas destroyed by earthquakes or tsunamis. They can find humans in the cold, heat, smoke, and dust. Rescue animals are amazing!"

1. He said Bonnie was **my** / **his** rescue dog.
2. He said that Bonnie helped **him** / **me** find lost climbers.
3. He said that **her** / **his** sense of smell was amazing.
4. He said that rescue dogs **can** / **could** find humans in difficult conditions.
5. He said that they **are** / **were** amazing!

D Match the reported speech to direct speech.

1. The tourist said that she was lost.
2. Hamid said that it was a long way home.
3. Ana and Yolanda said that they liked mountain climbing.
4. Mrs. Walsh said she was taking photos of the birds.
5. Mr. and Mrs. Nouri said that they didn't go hiking very often.
6. Farid said that he couldn't speak French.

a. "I can't speak French."
b. "I am lost!"
c. "We don't go hiking very often."
d. "It's a long way home."
e. "We like mountain climbing."
f. "I'm taking photos of the birds."

E What did Felix say to the mountain rescue team? Change from direct speech to reported speech.

1. "I don't like the rain," said Felix.
   Felix said that he didn't like the rain.
2. "I'm feeling very tired," he said.
   _____
3. "My ankle is swelling up and it is painful," he said.
   _____
4. "I have two friends with me," he said.
   _____
5. "They can't speak English," he said.
   _____
6. "We don't want to stay in the cave all night," he said.
   _____
7. "I want to get a message to my brother!" he said.
   _____

42 Unit 7 Rescue!

Reported Speech with *Said That*

F Complete the reported speech sentences. Use the information in the box. What did these people say?

> ~~"I'm delighted Felix is safe."~~   "I am very happy to be off the mountain!"
> "It's an exciting news story."   "I am happy that Bonnie, my rescue dog, can help."
> "It is a difficult place to land."   "Felix's ankle is fine."

1 Felix's brother said he was delighted Felix was safe.
2 The news reporter said that _____.
3 The doctor said that _____.
4 Marc, the rescue volunteer, said that he _____.
5 The mountain rescue helicopter pilot said _____.
6 Felix said he _____.

G Imagine you work in the mountain rescue office with Ian. Tell the story of Felix's accident.

Direct speech	Your accident report
1 "I can speak a little English."	Felix said that _____.
2 "My foot hurts."	He said that _____.
3 "I have two friends with me."	He said _____.
4 "I can't walk."	He _____.
5 "I need to be rescued!"	He _____.

✎ Let's Write!

H Interview your partner about an accident. What happened? What did everyone say? Draw pictures and then write the story underneath. Use reported speech.

My brother is three years old.

He likes running.

He runs everywhere, fast.

My brother said that his head hurts.

My mom said that she was worried.

We went to the hospital.

The doctor said that it was fine.

Everyone is happy.

> I spoke to …   She said …   He said …   Her mother said …   The police officer said …

Reported Speech with *Said That*   Rescue!   **Unit 7**   **43**

8 The Secret World of Ants

Discover Grammar

A Listen and read. The fourth grade are at the Rainforest Museum. 16

Guide	These are leafcutter ants. They're from Central and South America. They recycle about 20 percent of leaves in the rainforest.
Children	Wow!
Guide	They have lots of different jobs. There are soldier ants, scouts, leaf cutters, gardeners, and there is, of course, the queen.
Girl	How many of them live together?
Guide	Sometimes over five million ants live together in a nest. And they are really strong. They can carry over 50 times their own weight.
Boy	Can they talk to each other?
Guide	No, they can't talk, but they do communicate. They can warn each other when there's danger. And they tell each other where to find food. They use their antennae to pick up smells from other ants. The smells are called scents. They can leave about twenty different scent messages by rubbing their abdomen (their body) on the ground.

B The children are back at school. What do they remember? Match the questions and answers.

1 What did the guide tell us about leaves?
2 What did she say about their nests?
3 Did you ask any questions?
4 What did she say about communication?

a I asked her if the ants could talk to each other.
b She told us that the ants could leave about twenty different scent messages.
c She told us that the ants recycled about 20 percent of the leaves in the rainforest.
d She said that sometimes over five million ants lived together in a nest.

Reported Speech with *Told* and *Asked* • Reported Questions

C Look at the answers in **B**. Find the direct speech in the story and underline.

D Match the questions to the reported speech.

1 "What are the ants doing?"
2 "How many ants are there in the tank?"
3 "Which one is the queen ant?"
4 "When do the ants sleep?"

a We asked her when the ants slept.
b Antonio asked her what the ants were doing.
c Yolanda asked her which one the queen ant was.
d I asked her how many ants there were in the tank.

Learn Grammar

A Read and learn.

Learn Grammar — Reported Speech with *Told* and *Asked*

We use *said* in reported speech if we don't say who the person was talking to.
"Ants live in giant nests." → The guide **said** that ants lived in giant nests.

We use *told* in reported speech when we say who the person was talking to.
We use a name, an indefinite pronoun, or object pronoun.
The guide **told me** that the ants lived in giant nests.
The teacher **told everyone** that the bus was leaving.

TIP The object pronouns are *me, you, him, her, it, us, you, them*.

Reported Questions

For reported questions, use *asked* + name or object pronoun + *if* or *whether*. Remember to change the tense and change the question mark to a period.
"Do ants eat flowers?" → Farid asked **her if / whether** ants ate flowers.
"Can I leave the room?" → I asked **Leni if / whether** I could leave the room.

For reported questions with question words, change the word order back to a normal affirmative sentence.
"Where are the ants?" → I asked her **where** the ants **were**.
"What are they eating?" → She asked them **what** the ants **were eating**.

B Circle the correct verbs.

1 The principal **told** / **said** everyone about the insect competition.
2 Mrs. Ansell **told** / **said** that we could make models.
3 Gemma **told** / **said** me that she wanted to find a picture of a beetle.
4 Selma **told** / **said** the posters looked colorful.
5 I **told** / **said** the best one was Miranda's.
6 My mom and dad **told** / **said** my picture was fantastic.

Reported Speech with *Told* and *Asked* • Reported Questions

C Listen and read. Highlight all the examples of *said that*, *told ... that* and *asked ... if* in the text. 🔊 17

My Wolf Project

We went to the wildlife park this holiday. I talked to the keeper. His name was Mr. Andy Damon. Andy studies wolves. He said that wolves used their body language and their faces to communicate. He said that they used their ears, tails, and body position to share their feelings with the rest of the pack. I don't like the noise wolves make. He said that the noise was called a howl. I asked him if howling was a sign of anger. He told me that wolves howled to scare other animals away and to protect their young, but he also said that sometimes they probably just howled for fun!

D Complete the sentences. Write *said*, *told*, or *asked*.

1 Mr. Damon _____ me that he studied wolves.
2 He _____ that wolves used their bodies and faces to communicate.
3 I _____ him that I didn't like the noise wolves make.
4 I _____ him if howling was a sign of anger.
5 He _____ me wolves howled to scare other animals away.
6 He also _____ they howled for fun!

E Change the direct speech to reported speech.

1 "I'm doing my homework project."
Maria told Anton that she _____ homework project.

2 "Are you writing about wolves?"
Anton asked Maria _____ about wolves.

3 "Yes. I love wolves!"
Maria said that _____ wolves.

4 "I have a picture of them on my T-shirt."
Cristophe said that _____ a picture of them on _____ T-shirt.

5 "Can I copy your T-shirt?"
Maria asked Cristophe _____ T-shirt.

46 Unit 8 The Secret World of Ants

Reported Speech with *Told* and *Asked* • Reported Questions

F Change these questions into reported speech.

1 "Where is the wildlife show?"
He asked where _____.

2 "How many tickets do you have?"
She asked how many _____.

3 "What time does it start?"
They asked what _____.

4 "Can I sit near the front?"
He asked if _____.

5 "Do you want some ice cream?"
She asked whether _____.

6 "Can I take photos?"
They asked if _____.

G Read the sentences. Circle the speaker(s). Underline the listener(s).

1 (The attendant) asked if I could give my ticket to her.

2 Lucy told me the parrot gave her a strange look.

3 The guide asked me if I was listening to him.

4 The animal keepers told Oscar they were going to see his talk about birds.

5 You asked us if we had an information booklet.

6 Adam and Toby told Jake that he could sit with them.

H Match the direct speech to the sentences above. Write a number. Then complete the text.

___1___ "Can you give ___your___ ticket to ___me___?"
_____ "_____ are going to see _____ talk about birds."
_____ "Are you listening to _____?"
_____ "Do _____ have an information booklet?"
_____ "_____ can sit with _____."
_____ "The parrot gave _____ a strange look."

💬 Let's Talk!

I Talk to your partner about the insects, birds, and animals they like. Think of five questions to ask. Write them down. Use these ideas or your own.

- Do you like animals?
- Do you like going to the zoo?
- Do you think ants are smart?
- Which animals are you good at drawing?
- What is your favorite animal?

J Now talk to a different partner. Tell them about your questions, and what your first partner said to you. Use reported speech!

> I spoke to Amelia. She said that her favorite animal was an elephant. She told me she liked going to the zoo. I asked her if she thought ants were smart.

Module 4 Review

A Complete the sentences in reported speech.

1 "I'm learning about bees," said Jack.
   Jack _____ me that he was learning about bees.

2 "Are you drawing a picture?" I asked.
   I _____ if he was drawing a picture.

3 "I can't draw bees," he said.
   Jack said _____ couldn't draw bees.

4 "I can help you" I said.
   I told him _____ help him.

5 "How can you help me?" he asked.
   He _____.

6 "I draw fantastic insects …!" I said.
   I told _____.

Hot Spot How do you think bees choose which flowers to visit? Bees make a loud buzzing noise if they are disturbed. Why do you think they do this?

Learn Grammar — Time Words in Reported Speech

When you use reported speech, you need to change some words, such as time and place words.

here → there   this → that
now → then   next week → the next week
today → that day   tomorrow → the next day
tonight → that night this year → that year

Lisa: "There are five bees here in my garden today."

Lisa said there were five bees there in her garden that day.

B Complete the sentences. Change the tenses and use the correct time and place words.

1 "I'm visiting the wildlife park next week."
   She said that _____.

2 "I think this is really interesting."
   He said that _____.

3 "The weather is good for bees this year."
   Mom said that _____.

4 "I'm planting some purple flowers tomorrow."
   She said that _____.

9 Granny Stops Museum Thief!

Discover Grammar

A Listen and read. 18

The police thanked 86-year-old grandmother Mavis Jones yesterday for stopping a robbery at the City Art Museum. We interviewed Mavis:

Why did you go to the museum?
I went because it's nice and warm. I go there every afternoon.

Who did you go with?
I went by myself.

Where did you see the robber?
He was in the Italian art room, in a long black coat. I was suspicious. It was a sunny day. Why did he need a coat?

What did you do?
I hid behind a statue. I saw him take a painting and put it under his coat!

How did you stop him?
I shouted, "Hey! You stop that, young man!" He started to run. So I tripped him with my cane. Then I sat on him. I shouted, "Help, thief!" I have quite a loud voice, you know.

Who helped you?
The security guards! They ran in and rescued the picture. Then they called the police. It was very exciting!

Congratulations, Mavis. You are our hero!

B Read again and underline the question words.

C Act it out. Work with a partner. Practice asking the questions.

Asking Questions • Subject / Object Questions

Learn Grammar

 A Read and learn.

 Learn Grammar   **Asking Questions**

Questions which ask for information begin with question words: *what, where, when, why, who, whose, which, how*. The question word comes first, then a form of the verb *to be* or the auxiliary verb, and then the subject.

> **TIP** Auxiliary verbs are *have, will, would, can, could, shall, should, may, might,* and *must*.

The thief was in the art room. → **Where** was the thief?

And when there is no auxiliary verb, use *do* or *did* to make a question.

Mavis goes to the museum. → When **does** Mavis go to the museum?
They stopped the thief. → How **did** they stop the thief?

Subject / Object Questions

- Look at these sentences.
  Who stole the picture?   **The thief** stole the picture.
  What happened next?   **Something exciting** happened.
  Who stopped the thief?   **Mavis** stopped the thief.

  In the questions, the verb is the same as it is in the affirmative sentence, and the word order does not change. The question word is the subject of the affirmative sentence.

- Look at these sentences.
  Who did Mavis stop?   Mavis stopped **the thief**.
  (**Mavis** is the subject. **Who** is the object.)

In the question above, the question word is the object of the sentence.
Make the question with a form of *do*. Compare:
Somebody stopped the thief. Who?
Who stopped the thief? (**Who** is the subject.)

Mavis stopped somebody. Who?
Who did Mavis stop? (**Who** is the object.)

B Find the two questions with *Who* in the story. Write in the order you find them in the story.

1 _____

   Who is the object of the sentence.

2 _____

   Who is the subject of the sentence.

C Read the questions and answers. Choose the correct question words.

> What   Where   Who   Why   When

1 _____ is the museum? It's in the center of the city.
2 _____ likes to go there? Mavis does.
3 _____ does she usually go? She goes there every day, in the afternoon.
4 _____ does she do in the museum? She looks at the pictures.
5 _____ does she like it? Because the pictures are beautiful, and the museum is warm!

D Write the question words.

1 Mavis went to the museum.
_____ went to the museum?
_____ did Mavis go?

2 Mavis loves art.
_____ loves art?
_____ does Mavis love?

3 Picasso painted the picture.
_____ painted the picture?
_____ did Picasso paint?

4 The museum is next to the Town Hall.
_____ is the museum?
_____ is next to the Town Hall?

5 Mavis shouted loudly.
_____ shouted loudly?
_____ did she shout?

6 Everyone cheered Mavis!
_____ cheered Mavis?
_____ did everyone cheer?

E Reorder the words to make subject questions. Then match them to the answers. Read the story on page 49 again if you need help.

1 the / where / was / thief / ?
_____
2 watched / thief / the / who / ?
_____
3 ran / the / to / exit / who / ?
_____
4 her / for / help / thanked / who / Mavis / ?
_____
5 Mavis / who / helped / ?
_____

a Mavis watched him.
b In the Italian Art room.
c The security guards did.
d The thief did.
e The police did.

Asking Questions • Subject / Object Questions

Granny Stops Museum Thief!   Unit 9

F Listen and read. Complete with question words. Then listen again to check your answers. 🔊 19

Police officer	OK, everyone. Listen, please. Mavis Jones will answer questions now.
Journalist	¹ _____ do you go to the City Art Museum, Mrs. Jones?
Mavis	I go there every afternoon. It's my favorite place in town.
Journalist	² _____ did you stop the thief?
Mavis	I used my cane. And then I sat on top of him. I was really mad!
Journalist	³ _____ happened next?
Mavis	I called for help, and the security guards came in. They found the picture, and they helped me stand up!
Journalist	⁴ _____ called the police? You or the guards?
Mavis	The guards called the police. I don't have one of those cell phones.
Police officer	Thank you, everyone. That's all we have time for now …

G Underline the two subject questions and circle the two object questions in **F**.

H Read the sentences. Write questions with question words. Use *does*.

1 Where _____? Mavis lives near the City Art Museum.
2 When _____? She goes to the museum in the afternoon.
3 What _____? She looks at the Italian art.
4 Who _____? She doesn't meet anyone.

I Write questions. Ask about the words in *italics*.

1 Who used her cane? — *Mavis* used her cane.
2 What did she use to stop the thief? — Mavis used *her cane* to stop the thief.
3 _____ — *The thief* wore a long black coat.
4 _____ — The thief wore *a long black coat*.
5 _____ — The thief stole *a picture*.
6 _____ — *The thief* stole a picture.
7 _____ — *The security guards* helped Mavis.
8 _____ — The security guards helped *Mavis*.

💬 Let's Talk!

J Work with a partner. Interview your partner about a vacation. Write six questions to ask your partner. You can use *who, what, when, where, how*. Try to write both subject and object questions. Then take turns asking your questions. Use these ideas or your own.

- Who went with you on vacation?
- Where did you go?
- What did you see?

52 Unit 9 Granny Stops Museum Thief! Asking Questions • Subject / Object Questions

10 General Knowledge Quiz

Discover Grammar

A Listen and read. How good is your general knowledge? 🔊 20

Many families in the U.K. like to play quiz games. These games test people's general knowledge. If you have good general knowledge, it means you know a lot about many different subjects. For example, history, geography and math. Here are some general knowledge quiz questions.

Q: Is Melbourne the capital city of Australia?
A: No, it isn't. It's Canberra.

Q: Will the next Olympic Games be in Europe?
A: No, they won't.

Q: Did the Chinese invent fireworks?
A: Yes, they did.

Q: Are whales mammals?
A: Yes, they are.

Q: Are wolves extinct?
A: No, they aren't.

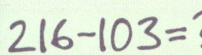
Q: Is 216 minus 103, 113?
A: Yes, it is.

B Underline the short answers.

C Act it out. Work with a partner and practice asking and answering the general knowledge questions.

Short Answers

Learn Grammar

 A Read and learn.

 Learn Grammar — Short Answers

In English, it's not always polite to answer a question with just "Yes" or "No".
Use short answers to be more polite.
Also, use short answers to yes / no questions to avoid repetition.
To make short answers, use the first verb from the question (to be or the auxiliary verb).

Question	Affirmative	Negative
Is this inventor Chinese?	Yes, he / she is ~~Chinese~~.	No, he / she isn't ~~Chinese~~.
Are whales mammals?	Yes, they are ~~mammals~~.	No, they aren't ~~mammals~~.
Will this invention change our lives?	Yes, it will.	No, it won't.
Do these animals live in Africa?	Yes, they do.	No, they don't.
Did you answer all of the questions?	Yes, I did.	No, I didn't.
Could the children do the quiz?	Yes, they could.	No, they couldn't.
Was that quiz question very difficult?	Yes, it was.	No, it wasn't.

TIP If you is the subject of the question, the short answer begins with I or we.

Question	Affirmative	Negative
Do you know the answer?	Yes, I / we do.	No, I / we don't.
Are you Mexican?	Yes, I am. (NOT ~~Yes, I'm.~~)	No, I'm not. (NOT ~~No, I amn't.~~)
But:	Yes, we are.	No, we aren't.

Use the long form (he does) in affirmative answers (yes).
Yes, I am.   Yes, they are.

Use the short form (he doesn't) in negative answers (no).
No, I can't.   No, we didn't.

B Read the questions and cross out the words in the answers that are not necessary.

1. Is Paris the capital of France?
   Yes, it is ~~the capital of France~~.
2. Did the dinosaurs die because of the cold?
   Yes, they did ~~die because of the cold~~.
3. Was Washington the first U.S. president?
   Yes, he was ~~the first U.S. president~~.
4. Will computers become smaller?
   Yes, they will ~~become smaller~~.
5. Did the Romans go to America?
   No, they didn't ~~go to America~~.
6. Were the first films in color?
   No, they weren't ~~in color~~.
7. Do people live on Mars?
   No, they don't ~~live on Mars~~.
8. Does the word "tiger" begin with the letter "t"?
   Yes, it does ~~begin with the letter "t."~~

C Circle the correct answers. Listen and check. 🔊 21

TV presenter OK, now it's the Smith family's turn. You have one minute to answer all five questions. Ready?
Smith family Yes.
TV presenter OK. Question number 1. Is Bogotá the capital of Colombia?
Smith family ¹ **Yes, it is. / Yes, it's.**
TV presenter Good. One point. OK, Question 2 now. Are kangaroos mammals?
Smith family ² **Yes, they are. / Yes, they're.**
TV presenter Correct. Well done. Question 3. Was Yuri Gagarin the first man to fly in space?
Smith family ³ **Yes, he wasn't. / Yes, he was.**
TV presenter Correct again. Question 4. Did Marlowe write *Hamlet*?
Smith family ⁴ **No, he didn't write. / No, he didn't.**
TV presenter Correct: of course, it was Shakespeare. And now the last question for tonight's prize of $1,000. Was the Internet a 1970s' invention?
Smith family ⁵ **No, it wasn't. / No, it was not.**
TV presenter ⁶ **Yes, it is! / Yes, it was!** Oh, I'm so sorry. People started using the Internet in 1976.
Smith family Oh, no!

D Look at the pictures and answer the questions with short answers.

1 Is Mount Kilimanjaro in Tanzania? _____
2 Do polar bears live in Alaska? _____
3 Will it be sunny tomorrow? _____
4 Was Tyrannosaurus Rex the biggest dinosaur? _____
5 Were the Vikings from Africa? _____

E Read the questions and write the correct short answers.

1 Do you like watching TV?   Yes, _____
2 Are you going out tonight?   Yes, _____
3 Did you watch TV last night?   No, _____
4 Will you finish your homework tonight?   No, _____
5 Were the quiz questions difficult?   No, _____

F Now write short answers to these questions which are true for you.

1 Are you ten years old? _____
2 Do you like sports? _____
3 Did you listen to music last night? _____
4 Will you get good grades on your next English test? _____
5 Were you in third grade last year? _____
6 Are you going to watch TV tonight? _____

Let's Write!

G Write a general knowledge quiz to test your friends. Write ten questions and ten short answers. Use these ideas or your own.

> Was Tchaikovsky a Russian composer?   Yes, he was.
> Is Berlin the capital of Germany?   Yes, it is.

Berlin

Pyotr Ilyich Tchaikovsky

Kangaroo

William Shakespeare

Yuri Gagarin

Unit 10 General Knowledge Quiz   Short Answers

Module 5 Review

A Read the fifth grade's web page about Sultan Suleiman, and complete the questions.

Sultan Suleiman lived in a palace called Topkapi Sarayi (Topkapi Palace) in Istanbul. Sultans lived there for about 400 years, from 1465 to 1856.

The palace is luxurious. It has marble floors, and beautiful tiles cover the walls. The Sultan's golden throne was decorated with precious stones.

Sultan Suleiman loved beautiful things. He lived in the palace with his family and his servants, and he ruled the country from here. He was a very important ruler.

Today, the palace is a famous tourist attraction.

1 _____ lived in the Topkapi Palace?
2 _____ did the Sultan live?
3 _____ lived there for 400 years?
4 _____ long did the Sultans live there for?
5 _____ covers the walls?
6 _____ do the tiles cover?
7 _____ else lived in the palace?
8 _____ did the Sultan's family and servants live?
9 _____ ruled the country from the palace?
10 _____ did the Sultan rule the country from?

B Write the answers to the questions in **A**.

C Read the questions and write true short answers for you.

1 Did you read the text in A? _____
2 Do you like the photo of the palace? _____
3 Could you answer all the questions in A? _____
4 Are you doing B at the moment? _____
5 Will you finish this activity soon? _____

Hot Spot What do you think it was like to visit the Sultan? Why? Would you like to live in a palace? Why, or why not?

11 Volcano

Discover Grammar

A Listen and read about Brendan, who studies volcanoes. 🔊 22

Brendan thinks it's important for scientists to tell people when a volcano isn't safe. He studies volcanoes so that people are told when it is dangerous in plenty of time.

Brendan has made a film about volcanoes. In the film, rocks inside the volcano melt. This is magma. Magma is pushed to the top of the volcano. The ground shakes. Suddenly rocks, magma, and hot gas explode into the sky. It's terrifying. People hear the noise from far away, even on other islands.

The eruption is so loud, the noise is heard a long way away. Hot lava travels down the mountain at 50 kph. Ash falls from the sky. The mountain is destroyed.

Brendan's work helps keep people safe. People living nearby are taken to safety, and no one is hurt. Their houses aren't damaged, but they are covered in ash. Their crops are buried. People can't return home for a year.

B Find and underline the past participles of these verbs in the text.

> tell   push   hear   destroy   damage   bury

C Look at the underlined past participles. Circle the verb that comes before each one. What do you notice?

---

58   Unit 11   Volcano

Passive: Simple Present Passive

Learn Grammar

A Read and learn.

Learn Grammar Passive

In English, we can often say things in two ways, using the active and the passive.
The ash buries the crops. (active)   The crops **are buried by the ash**. (passive)

We often put the most important information at the start of the sentence.
In the first sentence, the focus is on the ash. In the second sentence, the focus is on the crops.
Make the simple present passive with subject + *am / is / are* + past participle (*seen*, *played*, etc).

Affirmative
The noise **is heard** from far away.
People **are told** when it is dangerous.

Negative
Magma **isn't made** from gas.
Their houses **aren't damaged**.

Questions
Is the mountain **destroyed** by the volcano?
Are the people **taken** away by bus?

Short Answers
Yes, it is. / No, it isn't.
Yes, they are. / No, they aren't.

Use the passive when you don't know or it isn't important who or what does the action.
People **are taken** to safety.   (e.g. by helicopter)
Magma **is pushed** to the surface.   (by pressure in the mountain)

Use *by* to say who or what does the action.
People are asked to leave **by the police**.   Crops are buried **by the ash**.

Remember! You can't use some verbs (such as *cry*, *die*, *arrive*, *wait*) in the passive voice.

B Complete the sentences. Use the simple present passive.

1 People _____ (tell) when a volcano is dangerous.
2 Different scientific instruments _____ (use) to collect the data.
3 During an eruption, magma _____ (push) to the surface.
4 The noise _____ (hear) a long way away.
5 People _____ (take) to safety as quickly as possible.
6 Their homes _____ (damage), but they _____ (not destroy).
7 They _____ (not allow) to return home for a long time.
8 Their crops _____ (cover) in ash.

Passive: Simple Present Passive

C Read the text on page 58 again. Look at the information. Which sentences are true? Which are false? Correct any false sentences.

1 The mountain is destroyed by ~~the scientists~~. _____
2 The people are taken to a dangerous place. _____
3 The noise is heard by people a long way away. _____
4 Their homes are covered in lava. _____
5 Their crops are eaten. _____

D Read the sentences and circle the correct verbs.

1 This sensor **is checked** / **are checked** every hour.
2 We read the data. It **isn't given** / **aren't given** to the police until it is checked.
3 Tourists to the area **is asked** / **are asked** not to climb the mountain.
4 People **aren't sent** / **isn't sent** away unless it is too dangerous.
5 They **isn't allowed** / **aren't allowed** to drive near the volcano.
6 It's difficult when local people **are told** / **is told** to leave their homes.

E Complete the sentences using the correct form of the passive.

Hi there. I'm Eva Rojas. I'm a scientist. I work with Brendan at the Scientific Observatory. This is where reports ¹ _____ (write) and ² _____ (send) to the local police. Our job is to make sure the local people are safe. Have you ever wondered how volcanoes ³ _____ (measure)? We use a lot of different instruments, like seismographs, radio, and GPS devices. Gas samples ⁴ _____ (take) from cracks in the mountain. They are poisonous, so we must be very careful! Here's my latest report:

5:07 a.m.	The ground shakes. Magma ⁵ _____ (push) to the surface. Gases are escaping. Our instruments record a lot of activity. My boss ⁶ _____ (call) at home and he comes to the center right away.
6:12 a.m.	We are on red alert. Schools and farms nearby ⁷ _____ (close). People ⁸ _____ (not allow) near the area.
9:27 a.m.	Local people ⁹ _____ (tell) to leave their homes. Many ¹⁰ _____ (take) by bus to shelters in the next city. They won't be able to return for a few days.
3 days later	
7:48 a.m.	The volcano erupts. But thankfully, everyone is safe.

F Listen and check your answers. 🔊 23

Passive: Simple Present Passive

G Underline the verbs in the active sentences. Then change the sentences into the passive.

1. They <u>plant</u> many different crops in the soil.
   Many different crops are planted in the soil.
2. They grow grapes, beans and tomatoes in these fields.
   Grapes, beans, and tomatoes _____.
3. In other places, they grow rice on the rich volcanic land.
   In other places, rice _____.
4. They make electricity from the steam.
   Electricity _____.
5. They close the schools in the summer.
   The schools _____.
6. They need the children to work in the fields.
   Children _____.

Let's Talk!

H Look at the world map. It shows where some famous volcanoes are found. Find four volcanoes. Then tell your partner where they are found.

> Popocatepetl is found in Central America.

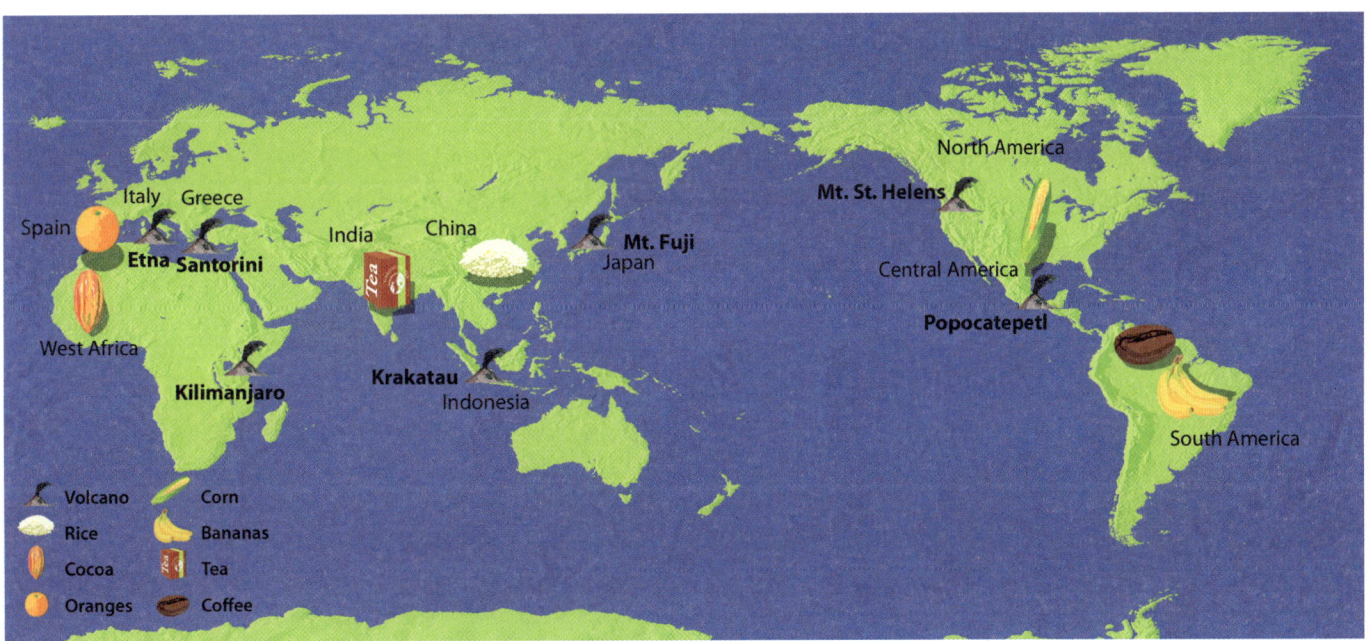

I The map also shows different crops which are grown in those areas.
Ask your partner where three different crops are grown.

> Where is rice grown?

> Where is cocoa found?

> Where are oranges grown?

Passive: Simple Present Passive

12 A Changed Landscape

Discover Grammar

A Listen and read. A journalist is interviewing the mayor about a village which was rebuilt to show life in the U.K. in the 1800s. 🔊 24

When was the village opened?

The idea was discussed in the 1950s by a group of librarians, and a collection of maps and old photos was started. In the 1970s, a plan was discussed to rebuild a village on a piece of land which had only old coal mines and empty factories. Work began soon afterwards and a few buildings were erected. Then in 1980, a tramline was installed to transport visitors to the center of the village.

Were lots of other buildings moved at that time?

Yes, they were. Lots of shops, houses, and factories were moved and rebuilt. Even a school, a movie theater, and a fairground were opened to the public.

Was everything moved at the same time?

No, it wasn't. The fairground and the movie theater weren't moved until later. It's very complicated. For example, all the bricks were numbered and photographed, and then they were put onto trucks and taken there.

Is the village complete now?

No, it is developing all the time. A complete 1930s street, for example, was added in 2010.

B Read again. Underline the past participles. Circle the verb that comes before each one. What do you notice?

---

62 Unit 12 A Changed Landscape

Passive: Simple Past Passive

Learn Grammar

 A Read and learn.

> **Learn Grammar** | Simple Past Passive
>
> Use the passive to emphasize the action or if you do not know who did the action.
> **When was the museum opened?**
> **It was opened in 1980.**
> **A 1930s street wasn't added until 2010.**
>
> Make the simple past passive with subject + *was / were* + past participle (*seen*, *played* etc).
> Affirmative: **The village was opened.**
> Negative: **The fairground and the movie theater weren't moved until later.**
> Questions: **Were lots of other buildings moved at that time?**
> **Yes, they were. / No, they weren't.**
>
> > **TIP** The past participle is often the same as the simple past form of the verb. However, some of the most common English verbs have irregular past participles, e.g. **eat → eaten; have → had; swim → swum**. There is a list on page 112. 
>
> Use *by* to show who did the action.
> **The idea was discussed in the 1950s by a group of librarians.**

B Complete the sentences. Use the simple past passive.

1 The wasteland _____ (change) to a tourist attraction.
2 Work on the village _____ (begin) in the 1970s.
3 All the bricks _____ (number and photograph).
4 A school _____ (rebuild).
5 The village _____ (not build) in the 1950s.
6 The 1930s houses _____ (not move) until 2010.

Passive: Simple Past Passive

C Write sentences with the simple past passive.

1 A collection of maps and old photos / start

2 A plan / discuss / to rebuild a village

3 A tramline / install / to transport visitors

4 Lots of shops, houses, and factories / rebuilt

5 A movie theater and a fairground / open / to the public

6 The bricks / take / to the village

D Change from active to passive.

1 They rebuilt the village.

2 They moved a school and a factory.

3 The librarians started the collection of maps and photos.

4 They didn't rebuild the buildings at the same time.

5 They didn't move the fairground and the movie theater until later.

6 They erected a few buildings in the 1970s.

E Write short answers to the *yes / no* questions.

1 Was the village opened in 1950? ✗

2 Was a plan discussed to rebuild the village in the 1970s? ✓

3 Were the fairground and the movie theater moved before the school? ✗

4 Were all the bricks photographed and numbered? ✓

5 Was the tramline installed to take visitors to the old coal mines? ✗

6 Was a complete 1930s street added in 2010? ✓

F Look at the two photos. Listen and complete the text about the history of Dubai, a city in U.A.E. 🔊 25

Dubai was changed very quickly. The desert ¹ _____ (make) into a modern city. Very tall buildings ² _____ (erect). The roads ³ _____ (construct) for cars, not for camels. Lots of hotels and restaurants ⁴ _____ (build) for visitors. Many foreign banks and shopping malls ⁵ _____ (open) there. Everything ⁶ _____ (design) to attract tourists and business people. In 2011, a tram system, called the Dubai Metro, ⁷ _____ (install) to transport people quickly around the city. It ⁸ _____ (open) by the Sheikh. Dubai ⁹ _____ (not build) for the present: it ¹⁰ _____ (design) for the future.

✏️ Let's Write!

G Write about an area that was changed in your school. Use the ideas below or your own.

> *Our old school garden was changed last year …*

`Passive: Simple Past Passive`   A Changed Landscape   **Unit 12**

Module 6 Review

A Match the text to the pictures. Write a number. Then highlight eleven simple present passives in the text.

Make your own volcano!

1 Two spoons of semolina and six spoons of bicarbonate of soda are put in a glass bottle. The bottle is shaken to mix them up.
2 A small glass is filled with vinegar. A few drops of red food coloring are added.
3 The bottle is taken outside and is put on the ground. Sand is piled up around the bottle like a mountain, until only the neck shows. This is the volcano.
4 A sheet of paper is used to make a funnel. The liquid is poured carefully into the bottle.
5 The volcano erupts!

Why does it erupt? Vinegar and bicarbonate of soda react together. Carbon dioxide is formed. Bubbles are formed. These bubbles push the semolina and food coloring out of the top of the bottle.

Hot Spot Would you like to be a scientist who studies volcanoes? Why, or why not?

B Make the simple present passive statements into questions.

1 Crops are grown on the volcanic soil. <u>Are crops grown on the volcanic soil?</u>
2 Magma is pushed up inside the mountain. _____
3 Information is collected. _____
4 The data is analyzed. _____
5 Samples of gas are collected. _____
6 Tourists are told not to climb the mountain. _____

C Read these reviews of the village and complete with past passive forms of the verbs in the box.

| build   change   make   take   offer   open   pay |

I remember when the first house ¹_____ in the park. The park ²_____ completely in the next few years, and it looks lovely now.

A café ³_____ in 2000. I ⁴_____ a job there. It was a great place to work. I ⁵_____ manager after a month and I ⁶_____ very well.

I ⁷_____ to the village for my birthday when I was ten. It was great.

66 Module 6 Review

13 A Rich Man's Fine Clothes

Discover Grammar

A Listen and read the first part of the story. 🔊 26

Mullah Nasruddin worked hard. He was tired and hungry after farming all day. There was a party that night at the rich man's house. Nasruddin didn't want to be late, so he didn't go home to change. As Nasruddin walked into town, he imagined all kinds of wonderful food: cold drinks, juicy olives, tasty chicken.

The rich man opened the door. He looked at Nasruddin's dirty work clothes and muddy shoes. He scowled at his visitor.

Nasruddin walked into the crowded room. Everyone wore beautiful clothes. The tables were covered with delicious food. But nobody spoke to Nasruddin.

Nasruddin went home. He changed, and put on his expensive coat. He ran back to the party.

B Find four adjectives in the story and the nouns they describe.

_____

_____

_____

_____

C What do you think happens next? Tell your partner.

D Listen and read the second part of the story. 🔊 27

The rich man happily welcomed his elegant visitor. He opened the door and said, "Come and eat!" Nasruddin walked slowly into the room. People smiled warmly at him.

Nasruddin quietly sat down. He took some bread, and said clearly, "Eat, coat, eat!" He put the bread in his coat pocket. He took some figs, and said, "Eat, coat!" and put them in the other pocket. People stared nervously at this man feeding his coat. Nasruddin calmly fed his coat some olives, chicken, and grapes. "Eat, coat, eat!"

Eventually the host ran over and asked politely, "Excuse me, Nasruddin. What are you doing?"

Adjectives and Adverbs

E Find six adverbs in the second part of the story and the verbs they describe.

_____   _____   _____
_____   _____   _____

F How do you think the story ends? Tell your partner.

G Listen and read the end of the story. 🔊 28

> Nasruddin said, "When I came here earlier, in my old farming clothes, no one would talk to me. But when I changed into this coat, suddenly everyone was friendly. So I realize that I am not welcome at this party, but my fine clothes are. And so, I am feeding my coat."

Learn Grammar

A Read and learn.

Learn Grammar — Adjectives and Adverbs

You usually put adjectives before nouns. Adjectives describe people and things.
He had muddy shoes.   **He wore dirty clothes.**
He imagined cold drinks and tasty chicken.

When you use the verb *to be*, or when you use sense verbs, put adjectives after the verb.
The party was fun.   **He felt tired and hungry.**

See Unit 15 for more information about this.

Adverbs describe verbs. Adverbs of manner tell us how something happens. They usually go after the verb.
He walked silently into the room.   **People smiled warmly at him.**

To form an adverb of manner, you usually add *-ly* to the adjective.
calm → calmly   careful → carefully   wise → wisely

TIP happy → happily   gentle → gently

Remember! Some adverbs are irregular.   good → well   fast → fast

These adverbs can only come after the verb: *well, hard, fast*
He went home fast. ✓   **He fast went home.** ✗

Adverbs of frequency tell us how often something happens. They go before most verbs, but **after** the verb *To Be*.
The rich man often has a party for the townspeople.
I'm never late for school.

These are adverbs of frequency: *always   usually   often   sometimes   never*

68 Unit 13 A Rich Man's Fine Clothes   Adjectives and Adverbs

B Change the adjectives into adverbs.

1 quick   _quickly_   5 good   _____
2 nervous _____   6 fast   _____
3 nice   _____   7 polite   _____
4 quiet   _____   8 careful _____

C Circle the correct words.

1 The rich man smiled **warm** / **warmly** at him.
2 Nasruddin entered the room **slow** / **slowly**.
3 They wore **beautiful** / **beautifully** clothes.
4 The food was **delicious** / **deliciously**.
5 The rich man talked **loud** / **loudly**.
6 Nasruddin sat down **quiet** / **quietly**.
7 The room was **noisy** / **noisily**.
8 The people were **polite** / **politely**.

D Reorder the words to make sentences.

1 picked / some / up / grapes / delicious / he
He picked up some delicious grapes.

2 drink / cold / had / he / a
_____

3 delicious / it / tasted
_____

4 in / pocket / juicy / he / put / his / chicken / the
_____

5 stared / nervously / the / guests
_____

6 over / the / man / rich / ran
_____

7 answered / politely / he
_____

8 my / feeding / I / am / coat / beautiful
_____

E Underline the adjectives. Then write sentences. Use adverbs and the verbs in parentheses.

1 The rich man has a <u>loud</u> voice. (talks)
The rich man talks loudly.

2 Nasruddin is a hard worker. (works)
_____

3 Soodabeh wore beautiful clothes. (dressed)
_____

4 Their singing was noisy. (sang)
_____

5 Nasruddin is a fast runner. (runs)
_____

6 The guest had a kind voice. (spoke)
_____

Adjectives and Adverbs   A Rich Man's Fine Clothes

F Underline the adverb of frequency in each sentence. Then rewrite the sentence, using the words in parentheses.

1. The rich man always has a party in the summer.
   (usually) _____
2. Nasruddin is always at the party.
   (never) _____
3. Nasruddin usually works in the fields until sunset.
   (always) _____
4. He doesn't often wear his fine clothes.
   (doesn't usually) _____
5. He sometimes eats tasty chicken and olives.
   (doesn't often) _____
6. Nasruddin is never late for a dinner party.
   (sometimes) _____

G Listen and read another story about Nasruddin. Fill in the missing adverbs and adjectives. 🔊 29

| cold | delicious | fast | fine | loudly | quickly | sick | suddenly | usually |

Nasruddin's wife always felt ill in the morning. She ¹_____ asked Nasruddin to give her a ²_____ drink of water. But today, she still felt ³_____. She didn't even want some ⁴_____ grapes. She asked Nasruddin to get a doctor. Nasruddin got dressed ⁵_____ and ran downstairs. His wife ⁶_____ shouted from the window, "Don't worry! I feel ⁷_____. I don't need a doctor after all."

Nasruddin ran ⁸_____ all the way to the doctor's house. He knocked ⁹_____ on the door. The doctor opened the door. Nasruddin said, "Doctor, my wife was sick this morning. She told me to get a doctor. When I left the house, she recovered, and told me that she didn't need a doctor. So I have come here to tell you that you don't need to come to my house."

✎ Let's Write!

H Think about a festival you have been to, or a party with family and friends. What was it like? What did you do?

Draw a picture of the room and then write six sentences. You can describe the food, the decorations, the place, the music, or the other children. Use these ideas or your own.

- There were beautiful decorations.
- I wore my pretty scarf.
- We ate delicious fruit and drank cold juice.
- We played games noisily.
- My friends danced happily.
- The grown-ups talked loudly.

14 How Could We Make Our School "Green"?

Discover Grammar

A Listen and read. 🔊 30

Ideas from fifth grade for the school board

Our school is not very "green" at the moment. If we did some simple things, we would save electricity and would save money. If the school board discussed our ideas and made the changes we suggest, our school would be the "greenest" in Mexico. We ask the school board to discuss our ideas and take action on the best ones.

- If we had classes four days a week, the school would use less electricity.
- If we always turned off the lights when we left a room, we would save money.
- If we stayed at home and had classes on the Internet, we would be able to close the school!
- If we didn't use books, we would save paper.
- If we closed the doors and windows in winter, we would save money on electricity.

B Circle the word *if*, and underline the word *would* in the text.

C Read the text again and match.

1 make changes   a use less electricity
2 don't use books   b save paper
3 turn off the lights   c the "greenest" school in Mexico
4 close the doors and windows   d save money
5 have classes four days a week   e save money on electricity

D Complete the sentences with *if* and *would*.

1 _____ we did some simple things, we _____ save electricity and money.

2 _____ the school board made the changes, our school _____ be the "greenest" in Mexico

(Unreal Conditional)   How Could We Make Our School "Green"? Unit 14 **71**

Learn Grammar

A Read and learn.

Learn Grammar — Unreal Conditional

Use unreal conditionals to talk about something that probably won't happen.
You can imagine something is different from the real situation now.
If we turned off the lights, we would save electricity.
(But we don't turn off the lights.)

Unreal conditionals have two clauses:

If clause	+	main clause
If + simple past	+	'd / would / wouldn't + verb
If we turned off the lights,		we would save electricity.
If we had classes four days a week,		the school would use less electricity.

The main clause can come first.
The school would use less electricity if we had classes four days a week.

When the *if* clause comes first, add a comma. When the *if* clause comes second, don't add a comma.

B Read the sentences and circle the correct answer.

1. If I **would be / was** a teacher, I'd tell my students about being green.
2. If the school was closed on Fridays, we **will / would** have longer weekends.
3. If we **walked / would walk** to school, we wouldn't need school buses.
4. If we **will recycle / recycled** paper and plastic, the school would be greener.
5. It **will / would** be greener if we used paper, not plastic, bags for our sandwiches.
6. We'd save water if we **turned / would turn** off the faucet after washing our hands.
7. It **will / would** be better if we used plastic bottles more than once.

C Listen and read. Complete the text with the words from the box. 🔊 31

| 'd use   if (x2)   'd save   had   wrote   wouldn't have   stayed   did   would be |

Leader The fifth grade has sent us lots of ideas how to make our school green and how to save money. Do you think they are good ideas?

Milly Yes, I do. If the school ¹_____ everything the fifth grade suggested, we ²_____ very green.

Tom No, not everything! I think some of the ideas are not very good. If students ³_____ classes online, we ⁴_____ a school at all!

Jane Yes, that's right, but maybe ⁵_____ students had classes three or four days a week, we ⁶_____ electricity!

Tom Yes, the school would save electricity if we had a shorter school week, but if students ⁷_____ at home, they ⁸_____ more electricity there.

Leader OK, thanks for your comments. I think now it would be a good idea ⁹_____ we all ¹⁰_____ down our ideas in time for our next meeting, OK?

Unit 14 How Could We Make Our School "Green"?   Unreal Conditional

D Read an email from a student to his friend in the U.K. Circle the correct words.

Hi William,

How are you? Fine, I hope.

My school is working on a big project to be the greenest school in Mexico. I think some of the ideas are very good, for example:

We **¹ 'd** / **will** save a lot of energy if we turned off lights and computers when we are not using them. If we **² walk** / **walked** to school, we would not need school buses. It would be better if we **³ used** / **use** plastic bottles more than once, and it **⁴ will** / **would** be greener if we had paper, not plastic, bags for our sandwiches.

I think one of the ideas is very bad, though. Some students in the fifth grade said that if we had cold showers after PE, we **⁵ wouldn't** / **won't** have to heat the water at all!

I could send you some more ideas if your school **⁶ will** / **would** be interested in being green.

I'll write again soon.

Greg

E What do the parents think? Match the beginnings and ends of the sentences.

1. If my son only went to school for three or four days a week,
2. If they used plastic water bottles more than once,
3. If there were no school buses,
4. If the classrooms were cold in the winter,
5. It would not be good

a. it would not be hygienic.
b. if the children worked at home on their computers all day.
c. the children would be sick more often.
d. I would have to stay at home with him.
e. I'd have to drive my daughter to school.

F Look and write unreal conditional sentences.

1. recycle our clothes / help other people
   If we recycled our clothes, we'd help other people.

2. cycle to school / save money

3. use less paper / save more trees

4. recycle more / have less garbage

5. pick up litter / have a tidier town

Unreal Conditional   How Could We Make Our School "Green"?

 **Let's Write!**

G Read the blog about virtual classes and answer the questions in full sentences.

What would you do if your school closed and you had lessons online at home?

Mariam, Dubai

If my school closed, I would get up early – at five o'clock – and I would do all my school work in the morning. If I finished my work by, say, eleven o'clock, I would spend the rest of the day with my friends. We would go to the gym and play sports. I would really like that!

Sammy, Brazil

I wouldn't like it if I had all my classes at home. I would be unhappy if I didn't see my friends every day. I would hate it if I always had to work on my own.

1 What would Sammy miss if he didn't go to school?
   He _____.
2 When would Mariam do her school work if she could choose?
   She _____.

H Write your own post for the blog. Use the ideas above or your own.

If my school closed and I had to do work on the Internet, I …

Module 7 Review

A Change the adjectives into adverbs.

1 kind _____
2 noisy _____
3 polite _____
4 careful _____
5 good _____
6 slow _____

B Put the words in the correct order to make sentences and questions.

1 festival / always / a / Do / you / ? / summer / have

2 eat / food / of / . / delicious / lot / We / a

3 always / . / is / concert / a / There

4 everyone / ? / clothes / Does / special / wear

5 beautifully / their / . / People / decorate / houses

6 usually / ? / there / Are / games

C Work in pairs and make a list of suggestions to make your classroom look better. Use the ideas in the box.

> posters or pictures on the walls   samples of students' work on display   a library corner
> a student notice board   a computer corner   a table with a display or models

If we put …

If we had …

If we made …

… we'd have a place to show classmates what we've made!

… the classrooms would look more interesting.

… more people would visit the library.

Now write a new suggestion. Use your own ideas.

_____
_____

15 A Visit to a Science Museum

Discover Grammar

A Listen and read Maxine's diary about her class sleepover at a science museum. 🔊 32

The trip to London was long. We felt excited, but our teachers looked tired. When we arrived, we had a snack, which tasted good. We ate quickly and went to a room where a scientist explained clearly what we were going to do.

Then we worked in groups and did experiments. In the first experiment, we had three buckets of water: one cold, one warm and one hot. We put our hands slowly into one bucket and then took them out quickly and put them into another. After putting your hands into the cold water, the warm water felt hot. After putting your hands into the hot water, it felt cold!

In the second experiment, we closed our eyes and smelled food. My food smelled sweet, and I guessed it was a cake.

In another experiment, they played songs very fast. All the words sounded different. It was impossible to understand them. The music sounded strange, as well.

We went to bed at ten and they turned off the lights. Everything looked scary in the dark.

B Underline all the sense verbs (*look*, *feel*, *sound*, *taste*, *smell*).

C Read the text again and circle the word after each sense verb.

1 We felt **excited** / **excitedly**.
2 Our teachers looked **tiredly** / **tired**.
3 The snack tasted **good** / **well**.
4 The warm water felt **hotly** / **hot**.
5 The food smelled **sweetly** / **sweet**.
6 The music sounded **strange** / **strangely**.
7 Everything looked **scarily** / **scary** in the dark.

D Complete the sentences with the adjectives or adverbs in the box.

| strange   quickly   sweet   clearly   slowly |

1 We ate the snack _____.
2 The cake smelled _____.
3 The scientist explained everything _____.
4 We put our hands _____ into a bucket.
5 The music sounded very _____.

76 Unit 15   A Visit to a Science Museum   Sense Verb + Adjective

Learn Grammar

A Read and learn.

Learn Grammar — Sense Verb + Adjective

Sense verbs are: *feel, look, smell, sound, taste*
Use sense verbs with adjectives to talk about personal opinions and thoughts about things and people.
The water **feels** warm.
You **look** tired.
Fresh bread **smells** fantastic!
This snack **tastes** delicious.
This new singer **sounds** original.

Use subject + sense verb + adjective.

Remember! You normally use an adverb after most verbs, but NOT after sense verbs.

He feels **good**. (adjective)   He works **well**. (adverb)
She looks **beautiful**. (adjective)   She plays **beautifully**. (adverb)

B Read what the scientist said to the children, and circle the correct words.

Hello, everybody. My name's Jack Field. I work here in the museum. I'm a scientist. Am I speaking ¹ **loudly / loud** enough? Can you all hear me ² **clear / clearly**? Good.

I am pleased to see that you all look so ³ **happily / happy**. That's a good start. Now, you are going to do lots of experiments this evening and tomorrow morning. Most of the experiments are about the senses, so we will be asking you to touch, smell, and listen to things. You will have to decide if something feels ⁴ **cold / coldly** or ⁵ **warm / warmly**. Or if something sounds ⁶ **loud / loudly** or ⁷ **quiet / quietly**. Or if a chemical smells ⁸ **bad / badly** or ⁹ **good / well**! We will also give you some things to eat, and you'll have to say if they taste ¹⁰ **sweet / sweetly** or ¹¹ **bitter / bitterly**.

We have lots of things for you to do, so it's important that you work ¹² **quickly / quick** and ¹³ **careful / carefully**. Let's make a start. Can you all now walk ¹⁴ **quiet / quietly** to the laboratory?

C Read the questions that the children have to answer for each experiment. There are eleven mistakes. Change the words to correct the mistakes.

> **Worksheet 2**
>
> **Experiment 4**
>
> Put your hands into the boxes and touch the animal skins quick.
> How do they feel? Which one feels coldly and roughly? Which one feels smoothly?
> Which one feels warmly?
>
> **Experiment 5**
>
> Listen careful to each noise.
> Which engine sounds very loudly? Which bell sounds very quietly?
>
> **Experiment 6**
>
> Close your eyes. Take a bite of each fruit and chew it slow. Which
> fruit tastes very sweetly? Which tastes bitterly? What are they?

D Complete the text with adjectives or adverbs from the boxes. There are six words that you won't need to use.

Adjectives | good cold loud horrible strange scary

Adverbs | well coldly loudly horribly strangely scarily

Jacky   Are you asleep, Mel?
Melanie No, I didn't sleep very ¹ _____. I felt very ² _____. The room was freezing.
Jacky   Me too. I heard lots of noises, and the air conditioning sounded very ³ _____.
Melanie Yes, it was very weird.
Jacky   And the air smelled ⁴ _____. Not like normal. I think it was from the chemicals we used in the experiments.
Melanie Yes, maybe. And in the dark, the objects in this room looked ⁵ _____. Like monsters! I was frightened.
Jacky   And my mouth felt ⁶ _____ because of all the bitter things they gave us to chew!

E Listen and check your answers. 🔊 33

F Reorder the words to make sentences.

1 good / our / tasted / sandwiches _____
2 felt / water / the / cold _____
3 bad / sounded / engine / car / the _____
4 the / children / tired / looked _____
5 horrible / chemicals / smelled / the _____

G Circle the correct verbs.

1 We all **tasted** / **felt** tired after the trip.
2 The singers **sounded** / **tasted** happy.
3 The food in the restaurant **sounded** / **tasted** good.
4 The museum **looked** / **smelled** scary in the dark.
5 The chemicals **felt** / **smelled** bad.

H Circle the correct words.

1 The scientist spoke **clearly** / **clear**.
2 The children waited **quiet** / **quietly**.
3 The teachers and the children looked **happy** / **happily**.
4 He **quickly** / **quick** put his hand into the water.
5 The air in the room smelled **sweet** / **sweetly** after the experiment.
6 We **slowly** / **slow** opened our eyes.

Let's Talk!

I Show a picture of your pet, or an animal you like, to your partner. Describe it. Does your partner agree with your description? Use these ideas or your own.

His ears look very soft.

His eyes look very friendly.

He makes noises with his trunk. It sounds funny.

He smells sweet.

No, they look rough to me.

They look sad to me.

I think it sounds too loud.

Oh no! I think he smells horrible.

Sense Verb + Adjective   A Visit to a Science Museum

16 At the Circus

Discover Grammar

A In Las Vegas, U.S., some international artists are performing in a show. Listen and read the interviews. 🔊 34

Michael Kanu from Senegal – tightrope and aerial dancing
Is it easy to be a circus performer?
It depends. Sometimes it's difficult to learn new routines, but it's fantastic to perform in front of an audience. It might look easy, but it's difficult to do well. I love performing, so it's fun to be onstage.

Olivia Chen from China – juggling
Do you like touring, or is it better to stay in one city?
I like touring, because it's interesting to visit new places. I like traveling. But my husband prefers being in one place, because it's tiring to travel all the time.

Selcuk Akpek from Turkey – acrobatics
What do you like most about being in the circus?
I love being part of this "international family": we come from all over the world, and we are great friends. When I first arrived, I couldn't understand much. My English wasn't very good, and it was hard to understand lots of different people, but now it's fine. This is the best job in the world.

B Read the interviews again. Find these adjectives and underline them.

> difficult   fantastic   interesting   tiring   hard

Now complete the phrases from the interviews.

1 It's difficult <u>to learn new routines.</u>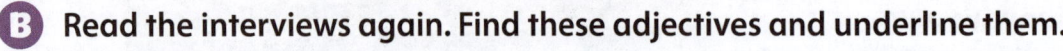
2 It's fantastic _____
3 It's difficult _____
4 It's interesting _____
5 It's tiring _____
6 It was hard _____

80   Unit 16   At the Circus   It's + Adjective + Infinitive

💬 Let's Talk!

C Read the interviews again. What do you think about their lives? Tell your partner.

I think it's _____ to be a circus performer because …

> … you can visit new places.

> … you travel all the time.

> … you have to do lots of training.

> … you might get hurt.

Learn Grammar

A Read and learn.

> ### 🔍 Learn Grammar — *It's* + Adjective + Infinitive
>
> Use *it's* + adjective + infinitive to give your opinions or to say what you think.
> **It's nice to meet** you.
> **It's easy to learn** how to juggle, but **it's difficult to do** it well!
> They speak so quickly, **it's impossible to understand** them!
>
> Use this pattern with adjectives such as *difficult, easy, hard, possible, impossible, right, wrong, nice, kind, clever, silly*.
> Use this pattern in questions, negatives, and with different tenses:
> Questions: **Is it hard to walk the tightrope?**
> Negative: **It isn't easy to perform seven nights a week.**
> Negative: **It isn't nice to fall over in front of the audience!**
> Past: **At the beginning, it was impossible to learn all the steps!**

It's + Adjective + Infinitive

B Listen and read the interview. Anita is the star of a new musical show called *Spaceship!* Then complete the text with the infinitives in the box. 🔊 35

| to be | to do | to have | to meet | to miss | to tell |

Hi Anita. It's <u>nice</u> ¹ _____ you. Congratulations on the show!
Thanks. It's a dream come true! It's hard ² _____ you how excited I am.

Do you get nervous onstage?
Yes. I've tried out for lots of other shows. Sometimes you are too short, too tall, your hair is the wrong color, or they don't like your voice. It's impossible ³ _____ perfect for every part. But then I got lucky! Wow! Spaceship! is great. It's fun ⁴ _____ things with your friends, and the other actors are my friends now.

Do you sometimes wish you were at home on the weekends?
Yes, I do. I love playing volleyball, and I can't play on my school team because of the show. It's disappointing ⁵ _____ birthday parties. But it's nice ⁶ _____ the chance to do this.

C Underline the adjectives in the interview. The first one has been done for you.

D Read the interview again. Match the two parts of the sentences.

1. It's nice — **a** to be perfect for every part.
2. It's disappointing — **b** to meet you.
3. It's impossible — **c** to miss birthday parties.
4. It's fun — **d** to have the chance to do this.
5. It's hard — **e** to do things with your friends.
6. It's nice — **f** to tell you how excited I am!

E Rewrite the sentences using *It's* + adjective + infinitive.

1. Working in the circus was fun.
   <u>It was fun to work in the circus.</u>
2. Training every day was hard.
   _____
3. In the beginning, remembering everything was impossible.
   _____
4. Being part of a team was nice.
   _____
5. Dressing up in a costume was fun.
   _____
6. Performing day after day was difficult.
   _____
7. Making children laugh every day was incredible!
   _____

Unit 16 At the Circus

It's + Adjective + Infinitive

F Correct the mistakes.

1 It's difficult ~~for~~ learn fire-eating.
   difficult to learn

2 It nice to perform every night.

3 It not interesting to stay in one city all the time.

4 I think it's nice to wearing a different costume for each new show.

5 It isn't hard for stay with the circus—it's the best job in the world for me!

6 It was interesting for travel to different cities each month.

G Write the questions.

1 Being onstage is scary.
   Is it scary to be onstage?

2 Learning your lines is difficult.

3 Missing parties is disappointing.

4 Meeting newspaper reporters is fun!

5 Saying what you miss the most is hard.

6 Having the chance to do this is nice.

H Change the sentences from affirmative to negative.

1 It's difficult to work with your friends.
   It isn't difficult to work with your friends.

2 It's scary to try something new!

3 It's easy to learn lines.

4 It's interesting to talk to reporters.

5 It's fun to miss school each week.

6 It's possible to be in every show.

✏️ Let's Write!

I Imagine that you work in the circus. Choose an act that you want to do, for example, tightrope-walking, fire-eating, or juggling. What do you do every day? What is your life like? Write about it. Use these ideas or your own.

- I work in the circus doing fire-eating.
- It's dangerous being a fire-eater!
- It's fun watching the audience when I'm fire-eating!

It's + Adjective + Infinitive

At the Circus   Unit 16

Module 8 Review

A Choose words from the box to complete Amy's report. There are two extra words.

> smelled   normally   feel   long   beautiful   normal   sounded   tasted   tired   ~~felt~~

I went to Disneyland near Tokyo with my family last weekend. It was a great trip, but I didn't enjoy the flight there. My brother and I ¹ _____felt_____ scared when the plane started to take off. We thought the noise of the engines ² _____ strange, but when the plane was in the air, the engines sounded ³ _____. The flight was only an hour, but it felt very ⁴ _____. We wanted to arrive as quickly as possible.

On the coach journey from the airport to Disneyland, our parents looked very ⁵ _____, and they soon fell asleep. When the coach arrived at Disneyland, we went to our hotel and unpacked quickly. There were some flowers on the table in our room. They looked ⁶ _____, and they ⁷ _____ fantastic.

Then we went to Disneyland and spent about five hours on the different rides and other activities. When I was younger, I used to ⁸ _____ sick on the rides in a fairground, but I loved all the rides at Disneyland. I'd like to go again one day.

Hot Spot Why do you think Amy and her brother were scared when the plane took off? What is your favorite way to travel? What do you like about it?

B Put the words in the correct order to make sentences and questions about the class trip to the science museum.

1 to / museum / It's / . / science / great / the / visit
   _____

2 experiments / do / Is / to / ? / interesting / it / the
   _____

3 understand / was / fast / difficult / It / . / songs / to / the
   _____

4 the / nice / It / taste / . / food / was / sweet / to
   _____

5 to / skins / strange / the / feel / It / was / . / animal
   _____

6 the / at / fun / to / Was / museum / ? / sleep / it
   _____

84   Module 8 Review

17 An Unusual Building

Discover Grammar

A Listen and read. Why is this building unusual? 🔊 36

Hi! My name's Jinghua. I'm thirteen and I'm a student. My favorite subject is art and my favorite sport is tennis. I want to be an architect one day.

I live in Harbin, in China. It's cold here, but I love snow! Every winter, there's a festival in Zhaolin Park. It's an international ice and snow festival. This year, I went to the festival with my family.

They take blocks of ice from the River Songhua and put them in the park. Artists turn the blocks of ice into palaces and statues. Visitors come from all over the world to see them.

I loved the ice palaces. My dad's an electrician. He told me that they use millions of bulbs to light up the buildings. I'm going to draw a picture of an ice palace later.

When spring comes, they take down the sculptures so the park doesn't flood. The blocks of ice are put back in the river. It's awesome!

B Find these sentences in the text. Circle the correct words.

1 I'm **a** / **the** student.
2 Every winter, there's **the** / **a** festival in Zhaolin Park.
3 I'm going to draw **a** / **the** picture.

C Find these sentences in the text. Complete the sentences with *a* or *the*.

1 I went to _____ festival with my family.
2 They take blocks of ice from _____ River Songhua.

D Find these sentences in the text. Cross out any extra words.

1 ~~The~~ my favorite subject is ~~the~~ art.
2 I live in the Harbin, in the China.
3 My favorite sport is a tennis.
4 Artists turn the blocks of ice into the palaces and the statues.

Articles: *A*, *An*, *The*, and No Article

Learn Grammar

 A Read and learn.

 Learn Grammar — A, An, The, and No Article

Use *a* and *an*:
- before singular countable nouns, when something is mentioned for the first time.
  There's a festival.
- for jobs.
  He's an electrician, I'm a student.
- with things that aren't special.
  I'm going to draw a picture of an ice palace. (This ice palace isn't special.)

Use *an* when a word begins with a vowel sound.
an international festival   an architect

Use *the*:
- with singular and plural nouns when both the speaker and listener know what we are talking about.
  I loved the ice palaces. (the ones in the park)
- when something is mentioned for the second time. We already know this information.
  There's a festival. (first mention)
  I went with my family to the festival. (second mention)

Don't use an article:
- before most country names and towns.
  I live in Harbin, in China. (BUT **the United States**)
- before plural nouns when talking about things in general.
  I like animals.
  Visitors come.
- with school subjects or sports.
  My favorite subject is art.
  I play tennis.

B Read and correct the sentences.

1. Jinghua is student.   —   Jinghua is a student.
2. She lives in the China.   _____
3. She went to international festival this year.   _____
4. A palaces were beautiful.   _____
5. She drew the picture of an ice palace.   _____

Articles: *A*, *An*, *The*, and No Article

C Complete the sentences with *a* or *an*.

1. Mr Lee is _____ designer.
2. She's _____ artist.
3. He's _____ electrician.
4. You're _____ interpreter.
5. Mrs Yu is _____ tour guide.
6. He's _____ truck driver.

D Complete the sentences. Circle *the* or – (no article). Then listen and check. 🔊 37

I'm from ¹ **the** / ⊖ New Zealand. I heard about the Harbin Ice and Snow Festival from my friend Chi. This year, we decided to visit ² **the** / – festival. It was great, and ³ **the** / – snow palaces were amazing. I like ⁴ **the** / – light shows, and ⁵ **the** / – lights here were awesome. At night, ⁶ **the** / – buildings shone with different colors. I'm really glad we went, and I want to go back to ⁷ **the** / – Harbin next year!

E Read the conversations. Circle *a* or *the*. Then listen and check. Act out with your partner. 🔊 38

Conversation 1

Let's go to Zhaolin Park. There's ¹ **a** / **the** festival today.

Really? Which one?

It's ² **an** / **the** annual ice and snow festival.

I'm not sure. I don't like ³ **a** / **the** snow.

It's awesome. You'll love it! We can see ⁴ **a** / **the** snow palaces made out of ice. They are amazing!

Really? OK. I'll get my camera. Let's go to ⁵ **a** / **the** festival!

Conversation 2

Wow! What's this?

I think it's ⁶ **a** / **the** magical fairy palace.

It's really beautiful. Look, we can go inside. Look up! Can you see ⁷ **a** / **the** lights?

They're really pretty. Let's go this way. I think that's ⁸ **a** / **the** exit.

Wait a minute. I want to take ⁹ **a** / **the** photograph. OK. Say "Cheese!"

F Match the two parts of the sentences. Then write the sentences with *a* / *an*, *the* or no article.

1. Shi Qi Gao is
2. He studies
3. He likes to visit
4. He wants to be
5. He thinks

a. ice and snow festival in Harbin every year.
b. student.
c. snow palaces at the festival are incredible.
d. art and technology in college.
e. architect when he finishes college.

1. Shi Qi Gao is a student.
2. _____
3. _____
4. _____
5. _____

Articles: *A*, *An*, *The*, and No Article

An Unusual Building **Unit 17** 87

G Complete the text with *a / an*, *the*, or no article.

Harbin is not the only place that holds ice and snow festivals. In Quebec, in ¹ _____ Canada, there is ² _____ Winter Carnival every year. There are shows, winter sports events, and snow and ice building competitions at ³ _____ Carnival, and there are parades through ⁴ _____ city every night. The opening ceremony takes place at ⁵ _____ Ice Palace. It's great fun, and everyone has ⁶ _____ amazing time!

💬 Let's Talk!

H Work in small groups. Imagine that you are going to an ice and snow festival. Design an ice building poster together. Label the picture.

Display your design in the classroom. Tell the other groups about your design. Think about using *a, an, the,* or no article when you speak!

> This is a snow school. It's got a snow playground and snow swings.
> In the playground, there are ...
> There are two classrooms. The classrooms have ...

> This is our snow hotel. It's awesome! It's got an ice restaurant.
> In the restaurant, you can see ...
> There's a snow gym. It's got a mirror made of ice!

18 The Castle

Discover Grammar

A Listen and read the story about Tom. He is twelve years old and he lives in a castle. 🔊 39

My name is Tom. I'm the baker's son. I work in the castle kitchen. Today is a special day. There's going to be a royal banquet tonight to celebrate the king's visit. He's arriving at six o'clock with the queen, and we are all excited and scared. Everyone has worked hard to get everything ready. We've cooked fish, meat, and sauces. We've prepared special fruit and drinks.

Last night, I was baking bread until very late, and my young brother Jack was cleaning the floors for hours. We were really tired this morning, but now we feel full of energy and excitement! I'm making a pudding at the moment, and later I have to help the cook take the dishes to the Great Hall. I think I'll have a chance to taste some of the food later. It all smells wonderful, and I have been hungry all day. I think the king will like my bread!

B Circle the tense that matches the story.

1 The king **will arrive** / **'s arriving** at six o'clock.
2 I'm a baker's son and I **work** / **have worked** in the castle kitchen.
3 I **am** / **have been** hungry all day.
4 Jack **cleaned** / **was cleaning** the floors for hours.
5 I **'m making** / **make** a pudding at the moment.
6 This morning, everyone **was** / **has been** tired, but now we feel full of energy and excitement!

C 1 Find three examples of different future forms in the story.

_____   _____   _____

2 Find three examples of different past tenses in the story.

_____   _____   _____

3 Find three examples of different present tenses in the story.

_____   _____   _____

Review of Tenses: Past and Present, Present Perfect and Future

Learn Grammar

A Read and learn.

Learn Grammar — Review of Tenses

Past

Use the simple past to talk about things that are finished.
I **worked** hard last night.   We **didn't have** much time.   **Did** everyone **cook** something?

Use the past continuous to talk about actions that were happening at a certain time in the past.
I **was working** in the kitchen.   She **wasn't listening** to me.
Were they **cleaning** the floor?

Present

Use the simple present to talk about facts and routines.
We **live** in a castle.   He **doesn't work** on the farm.   **Does** she **make** clothes?

Use the present continuous to talk about things that are happening now.
She **is making** bread.   He **isn't entertaining** the king.   **Are** they **dancing** for the queen?

Present Perfect

Use the present perfect to talk about actions that started in the past and are still happening now.
I**'ve been** hungry all day.   She **hasn't stopped** cooking.   **Have** you nearly **finished**?

Use the present perfect to talk about actions that have recently been completed.
I**'ve washed** the bowls.   I **haven't cleaned** the floor.   **Have** you **made** the soup?

Future

Use *going to* to talk about future plans and predictions about things we can see.
I**'m going to listen** to the music.   We **aren't going to dance**.   **Are** they **going to visit** us?

Use *will / won't* to talk about future facts and to make predictions about things you believe.
I think they **will enjoy** the meal.   He **will dance** tonight.   **Will** they **know** the answer?

Use the present continuous to talk about future arrangements.
He**'s arriving** at six o'clock.   I**'m going** to the cinema tomorrow.
Are you **meeting** her later?

B Reorder the words to make simple present sentences.

1 There / all over the world / many castles / are

2 different designs / have / They

3 round towers / Some castles / have

4 have / Many castles / strong walls

5 Most castles / cold and damp inside / are

C Make the present continuous sentences negative.

1 The knights are riding the horses.
_____
2 The jester is making the king laugh.
_____
3 The cook is preparing a great banquet.
_____
4 The peasant is working in the fields.
_____
5 The queen is eating her breakfast.
_____
6 The king is arriving at 6 o'clock.
_____
7 The baker is baking bread.
_____

D Listen and read. Complete the text using the simple past of the verbs in parentheses. Listen again to check your answers. 🔊 40

Farming ¹ ___was___ (is) very important to the castle inhabitants. Everyone who ² _____ (live) and ³ _____ (work) in the castle ⁴ _____ (need) food and drink, and so ⁵ _____ (do) all the animals. People ⁶ _____ (grow) most of their food in the fields around the castle. Inside the castle, the kitchen ⁷ _____ (is) an important room. It ⁸ _____ (contain) the fires for cooking. Castles usually ⁹ _____ (have) other rooms for food nearby, such as the bakery, and rooms where the cook ¹⁰ _____ (store) food.

E Complete the text using the past continuous. Listen and check your answers. 🔊 41

"I ¹ __was working__ (work) hard all day today. While the lords and ladies ² _____ (have) their main meal at eleven in the morning, we ³ _____ (work) in the kitchen, cooking for the dinner that night. The servants ⁴ _____ (clean) the bowls and jugs, others ⁵ _____ (light) the fires around the castle and the musicians ⁶ _____ (practice) their music. Imagine the noise!"

F Which jobs have the servants finished? Complete the sentences.

1 ✓ bake the bread (He) — He has baked the bread.
2 ✗ finish the pudding (They) — They haven't finished the pudding.
3 ✗ make the fires (She) — _____
4 ✓ pour the drinks (They) — _____
5 ✓ help the lady choose her clothes (She) — _____
6 ✗ clean the floor (He) — _____
7 ✗ cook the meat (She) — _____
8 ✗ feed the animals (He) — _____

Review of Tenses: Past and Present, Present Perfect and Future

G Complete the conversations between Tom and the cook. Choose questions from the box. Listen and check your answers. 🔊 42

> ~~Can you help me?~~   Is there going to be enough bread for everyone?   Do you think everyone will enjoy the banquet?   Did you light the fires?   Will it be good for the king?   Have you baked the bread?   Will you tell me when they arrive?

Conversation 1

Cook Tom, we need to check everything for the banquet tonight.
¹ _____Can you help me?_____

Tom Yes, certainly.

Cook ² _____

Tom Yes, I have.

Cook ³ _____

Tom Yes, it will. I think it'll taste delicious.

Cook ⁴ _____

Tom Yes, there is. We have cooked a lot.

Conversation 2

Cook The king and queen are going to be here soon. ⁵ _____

Tom Yes, I will. My friends are watching from the tower.

Cook Is it warm in the Great Hall?
⁶ _____

Tom Yes, I lit them all this afternoon.

Cook Good. ⁷ _____
_____

Tom Yes, I do. I think it'll be a wonderful banquet.

Cook Yes, me too!

H Act out the conversations with your partner.

✏️ Let's Write!

I Imagine that you live in a castle and you are a knight, a lady-in-waiting, a jester, a musician, or a cook. The king and queen are coming tonight for a banquet. How do you feel? What do you hope will happen? What are you going to do to get ready? What have you already finished?

Write your story. Start like this:

> *Today is a special day. The king and queen are going to visit the castle.*

I feel …	excited / scared / happy
I hope I will …	meet the queen / make them smile / prepare something delicious
Yesterday, I …	planned the menu / wrote a new song / polished my armor
I'm going to …	play the flute / cook the meat / wear special clothes / perform a new dance

Put your stories around the classroom for everyone to enjoy.

Module 9 Review

A Complete the text with *a / an*, *the*, or – (no article).

Tom lives in ¹ _____ castle. His dad is the baker at ² _____ castle and they're having ³ _____ banquet there tonight. It'll be ⁴ _____ amazing meal with ⁵ _____ meat, fish, and different sauces. Tom's making ⁶ _____ pudding at the moment and later he'll help take ⁷ _____ pudding and other dishes to the Great Hall. They often have banquets in ⁸ _____ June.

B Complete the text with the simple past of the verbs in parentheses.

They ¹ _____ (not have) the Internet in the castle! What ² _____ (they/do)? Well, everybody ³ _____ (enjoy) games and sports in the castle. People ⁴ _____ (play) board games, ⁵ _____ (tell) stories, and ⁶ _____ (listen) to musicians. The castle gardens ⁷ _____ (be) pleasant places to go for a walk.

C Match the two parts of each sentence.

1. I was cooking food
2. She was picking apples
3. He was feeding the horses
4. I was keeping a lookout
5. They were farming

a. from the watch tower.
b. in the kitchen.
c. in the stable.
d. in the fields.
e. from the trees in the garden.

D Put the words in the correct order to make sentences.

1. the banquet / arrived / The king / has / for
   _____

2. down / The queen / sat / has
   _____

3. hasn't / the kitchen / The food / from / come
   _____

4. started / play / The musicians / to / have
   _____

5. have / The singers / arrived
   _____

6. just / has / The banquet / begun!
   _____

E Circle the correct verbs.

Today is a special day. The princess ¹ **is / was** getting married. The king and queen ² **are / have been** delighted. There will be a royal banquet in the Great Hall tonight. The cook has been planning this meal for months. He ³ **is going to / will** cook a special menu with meat, fish, and fruit.

I think the Great Hall ⁴ **is going to / will** look spectacular. There are flags everywhere. We ⁵ **'re going to / will** wear our best clothes and jewelry. The musicians ⁶ **have written / were writing** some special new songs to play, and there will be dancing, too. I really hope that I can taste some of the cook's new recipes!

Exam Time

Unit 1

A Complete the interview between a boy and a woman who works at a safari park. What does the woman say? Write the correct letter (*a–h*).

Boy	Do you like your job in the safari park?
Woman	0 __c__
Boy	Have you worked in many other safari parks?
Woman	1 _____
Boy	Where else have you worked?
Woman	2 _____
Boy	Have you been to Africa or India?
Woman	3 _____
Boy	What jobs have you done in the safari park?
Woman	4 _____
Boy	Really! And have you ever been in danger?
Woman	5 _____
Boy	Oh!

a Oh, I've done lots of jobs here. So many over the years!
b I've worked in safari parks in England and France.
c Yes, I do. I like it very much.
d Yes, I have.
e No, I haven't. I've never seen the animals in the wild.
f I've never fed the tigers.
g Yes, I have. A tiger attacked me once!
h I love being with the animals.

B Complete the five conversations between two friends. Circle *a*, *b* or *c*.

0 Hello, how are you?
  (a) Fine, thanks.
  b Yes, I am.
  c Yes, please.

1 What have you been doing during the vacation?
  a I've been working at the park.
  b I'm working at the park.
  c I work at the park.

2 What work have you been doing?
  a I'm helping my dad.
  b I helped my dad.
  c I've been helping my dad.

3 How have you been helping him?
   a We are building a new play area together.
   b We've been building a new play area together.
   c We were building a new play area together.

4 Great! Have you been working with anybody else?
   a Yes, we were working with some builders.
   b Yes, we've been working with some builders.
   c Yes, we are working with some builders.

5 What have they been building?
   a They are building an area for small animals.
   b They have been building an area for small animals.
   c They were building an area for small animals.

Unit 2

Read the article about Greenpeace. Write the best word (*a*, *b* or *c*) for each space.

My parents ⁰ __c__ members of Greenpeace for years—since 1986. They ¹ _____ when they were students. When they ² _____ young, they liked the Greenpeace ships and balloons. ³ _____ any photos of them? Their most famous ship is called *Rainbow Warrior*. It ⁴ _____ great!

When I was younger, I ⁵ _____ how important Greenpeace is but now I do. Greenpeace started in 1971 and they ⁶ _____ one of the most important organizations in the world for conservation. They've campaigned to protect the rainforests and the oceans, and the whales. At the moment, they ⁷ _____ in Mauritius to stop the overfishing of tuna. Their work ⁸ _____ in forty countries all over the world.

0	a were	b are	c have been
1	a joined	b have joined	c join
2	a are	b were	c have been
3	a Did you see	b Do you see	c Have you seen
4	a has looked	b is looking	c looks
5	a didn't understand	b haven't understood	c don't understand
6	a became	b are becoming	c have become
7	a work	b worked	c are working
8	a is continuing	b continues	c has continued

Unit 3

A You saw these notices last week when you were on holiday in Greece. Match what you said (1–5) to the notices (a–h).

0 We couldn't play soccer there.
1 We could park there.
2 We could eat there in the middle of the day.
3 We could drive there at the weekend.
4 We couldn't swim there.
5 We couldn't buy cheap things there on Thursday.

a Danger! Deep water
b Museum shop – sale ends Wednesday!
c Swimming pool and gym open Mon–Fri
d Café open from 12:00–3:00p.m.
e Car park open. Please buy a ticket from the machine.
f No ball games allowed in the park
g This way to the dinosaur exhibition
h Road closed until Friday

B Look at the calendar and read the sentences. Write the correct dates.

0 We won't be able to go to the museum on that day. We're going to a party. ____June 5____
1 We'll be able to go to the cinema in the evening, after soccer. _____
2 We won't be able to go swimming then. _____
3 We won't be able to do our presentation then. There's a school trip. _____
4 We'll be able to work in the new Resource Center then. _____
5 We'll be able to go to the park after the tennis class. _____
6 We won't be able to go to the café then. _____
7 We won't be able to stay late after school that night. _____
8 We'll be able to do our homework together on Thursday, before Film Club. _____

June

M	T	W	T	F	S	S
30	31	01	02 Film Club	03	04	05 Party
06 Café Closed	07	08	09	10 Five a side soccer training	11	12 Trip to London
13 Pool closed	14	15	16	17 Resource Center opens	18	19
20	21 Governors meeting – school closed this evening!	22	23	24	25 Class at tennis club	26
27	28	29	30	01	02	03

96 Exam Time

Unit 4

A Complete the conversation between a man on a TV show and an antiques expert. What does the expert say? Write the correct letter (a–h).

Man   Could you say what this is? Is it a Roman plate?
Expert 0 __d__
Man   Oh yes. I see now! And is this ring valuable?
Expert 1 _____
Man   And I have another ring here. What do you think of this?
Expert 2 _____
Man   And here are some old coins.
Expert 3 _____
Man   And is this wooden toy very old?
Expert 4 _____
Man   I also have these old green bottles. Are they worth anything?
Expert 5 _____
Man   Thanks very much for your advice.
Expert You're welcome.

a Well, this ring must be worth a lot of money. It has three big diamonds in it.
b Yes, it might be valuable. It looks like a gold ring, but I'm not completely sure.
c These might be worth a lot of money, too. They are old German coins made of silver.
d No, it can't be Roman. It's made of plastic.
e I'm not sure. They might be. Some green bottles like this can be expensive.
f I am sure it is worth a lot of money. It was painted a hundred years ago.
g They can't be very valuable. They were made in a factory.
h Yes, it must be over 150 years old. It's a toy from the time of Queen Victoria.

B Answer the questions. Circle *a*, *b* or *c*.

1 Is this ring expensive?
   a Yes, it might. It's made of plastic.
   b Yes, it must be. It's made of plastic.
   c No, it can't be. It's made of plastic.

2 Are these toys worth a lot of money?
   a They can't be, but I'm not sure.
   b They must be, but I'm not sure.
   c They might be, but I'm not sure.

3 Is this coin very old?
   a No, it can't be. It has Roman writing on it.
   b Yes, it must be. It has Roman writing on it.
   c Yes, it might be. It has Roman writing on it.

4 Is this vase valuable?
   a It must be. Look—it's made of gold!
   b It can't be. Look—it's made of gold!
   c It might be. Look—it's made of gold!

Exam Time 97

Unit 5

A Read the article about teenagers' rooms in the future.
Are sentences 1–7 right (circle *a*) or wrong (circle *b*)? If there is not enough information to answer right or wrong, choose *Doesn't say* (circle *c*).

What will teenagers' rooms be like in twenty years? Scientists say that most rooms will have a robot. It will be like a personal assistant. The robot will do lots of jobs. For example, it will help teenagers do their homework, and write emails and texts. Of course, it will also make the bed and put clothes away.

The color of the walls will also change every day and computers will project different pictures, like posters, on the walls. Some teenagers' rooms will also have their own smart refrigerator, which will order drinks and snacks online when necessary. The typical bed of the future will have a personal movie screen and music system.

Parents predict that their teenagers will be very happy in such rooms, and teenagers say they will be over the moon!

0 Most rooms will have a robot.
 (a) Right   **b** Wrong   **c** Doesn't say

1 The robot will help in many ways.
 a Right   **b** Wrong   **c** Doesn't say

2 The robot will clean the room.
 a Right   **b** Wrong   **c** Doesn't say

3 It will help teenagers with their school work.
 a Right   **b** Wrong   **c** Doesn't say

4 Every week the walls will be a different color.
 a Right   **b** Wrong   **c** Doesn't say

5 All teenagers will have a smart refrigerator.
 a Right   **b** Wrong   **c** Doesn't say

6 A normal bed in the future will have a movie screen and music system.
 a Right   **b** Wrong   **c** Doesn't say

7 Parents think that their teenage children will be very happy with the room of the future.
 a Right   **b** Wrong   **c** Doesn't say

B Complete the sentences. Circle *a* or *b*.

1 Look at that black cloud. I think …
 (a) it's going to rain.
 b it will rain.

2 Next week, …
 a I'm flying to New York.
 b I will fly to New York.

3 This new car …
 a will travel at 300 kph.
 b is going to travel at 300 kph.

Unit 6

A Complete the conversation between two friends.
What does Greg say to William? Write the correct letter (a–h).

William	What are you doing at the weekend?
Greg	0 __c__
William	And what are you doing on Saturday afternoon?
Greg	1 _____
William	Are you going anywhere on Sunday?
Greg	2 _____
William	Are you doing anything special at home?
Greg	3 _____
William	Two hours of homework!?
Greg	4 _____
William	And Sunday afternoon? What are you doing then?
Greg	5 _____

a I'm doing my homework from about nine till eleven.
b My aunt and uncle are coming to visit us after lunch on Sunday.
c I'm playing soccer in the park on Saturday morning.
d My cousin is coming round on Friday evening.
e I'm probably staying at home on Sunday.
f It will probably rain all weekend.
g After the match, I'm going to my grandma's.
h Yes, I'm writing a project for science.

B Read Jack's diary. Circle *a* or *b*.

Monday	Go with Sara and Tom to Film Club
Wednesday	Play football
Thursday	Do history project after school
Friday	Go to school disco

1 **(a)** Jack isn't going to Film Club on Tuesday.
  b Jack won't go to Film Club on Tuesday.
2 a He will play football on Wednesday evening.
  b He is playing football on Wednesday evening.
3 a He will do his history project after school on Thursday.
  b He is doing his history project after school on Thursday.
4 a He is going to the school disco on Friday.
  b He will go to the school disco on Friday.

Exam Time

Unit 7

A Your friend told you about these notices. Match what your friend said (1–5) to the notices (a–h).

0   Your friend said that only blind people could take their dogs there.
1   Your friend told you that the bus didn't stop there any more.
2   Your friend said that you shouldn't take your dog for a walk there.
3   Your friend said that you would have to come part of the way by bus on Sunday.
4   Your friend told you that the times of the trains changed in the spring.
5   Your friend told you that he had seen a road accident.

a   Do not exercise dogs on the school field.
b   New train timetable starts from April 21.
c   Please have the correct change ready for the bus driver.
d   Bus stop not in use.
e   Make sure you take all your belongings with you when you leave the train.
f   No dogs except guide dogs.
g   Did you see a car accident here on Sunday March 4? Please call 01232 654093.
h   Engineering works on train line on Sunday. Buses will operate between Polegate and Lewes.

B Match the reported speech (1–5) to the direct speech (a–f).

1   "I'm hungry!"
2   "Let's begin the lesson, please!"
3   "I can't hear you!"
4   "I like playing football."
5   "We are listening."
6   "I'm drawing a picture of my classmates."

a   The teacher told us it was time to start.
b   Miranda said that she felt hungry.
c   Jack said that he liked playing football.
d   Sarah said that she was drawing a picture of her classmates.
e   Amy told me that she couldn't hear.
f   The students said that they were listening.

C Complete the second sentence using reported speech. Write a, b or c.

1   "I am lost!"   He said that he __a__ lost.
    a   was   b   were   c   did

2   "We are feeling cold."   They said that they ____ cold.
    a   feeling   b   were feeling   c   have feeling

3   "I can't see anyone."   She said she ____ see anyone.
    a   couldn't   b   wouldn't   c   didn't

4   "I am scared."   He said that ____ was scared.
    a   I   b   they   c   he

5   "My bag is heavy."   He said that ____ bag was heavy.
    a   my   b   your   c   his

100   Exam Time

Unit 8

A Complete the conversation between two friends. What does Rachel say to James about her visit to a castle? Write the correct letter (*a–h*).

James	What did the guide say about the castle?
Rachel	0 __f__
James	Did she tell you who built it?
Rachel	1 _____
James	Did she talk about any battles?
Rachel	2 _____
James	Did you ask any questions?
Rachel	3 _____
James	And what did she tell you?
Rachel	4 _____
James	Did you ask about the clothes they wore?
Rachel	5 _____

a Yes, she said they wore very warm clothes because it was very cold in the castle, even in the summer.
b She told me that they hunted deer and rabbits.
c She asked if the Normans kept animals in the castle.
d Yes, she said the Normans built it.
e Yes, I asked her if they hunted wild animals in the woods near the castle.
f She said it was 900 years old.
g She told me the Normans spoke French.
h Yes, she told me about the Battle of Hastings.

B Fill in the blanks. Write *a*, *b* or *c*.

1 The assistant __b__ me that the birds were very rare.
   a said   b told   c asked

2 I _____ her that I liked the yellow and blue ones.
   a said   b told   c asked

3 We _____ her if they came from another country.
   a said   b told   c asked

4 She _____ that they came from the South American rainforests.
   a said   b told   c asked

5 I _____ her if I could take a photo to show my sister.
   a said   b told   c asked

6 She _____ that it was OK.
   a said   b told   c asked

Exam Time

Unit 9

A Complete the interview between a police officer and a man who saw a car accident. What does the man say to the police officer about the accident? Write the correct letter (a–h).

Police officer	When did the accident happen?
Man	0 __b__
Police officer	And where were you when it happened?
Man	1 _____
Police officer	How did the accident happen?
Man	2 _____
Police officer	And could you see the drivers? What were they doing?
Man	3 _____
Police officer	Who caused the accident in your opinion?
Man	4 _____
Police officer	Who else saw the accident?
Man	5 _____

a Lots of other people were in the street at the time.
b It happened at four thirty two in the morning exactly. I checked my watch when I heard the bang.
c I was standing at the corner of the street.
d I was sitting at home watching the TV.
e Yes. The man driving the red car was texting. He didn't see the white car.
f Obviously the man who was texting. He wasn't paying attention.
g Nobody else saw it. I was alone in the street.
h The driver of the red car drove into the side of the white car.

B Complete the questions. Write *a*, *b* or *c*.

1 __c__ was the accident?
   In the street outside my home.
   a Who   b When   c Where

2 _____ was the driver doing?
   He was using his cell phone.
   a Where   b What   c Why

3 _____ did he crash?
   Because he wasn't driving carefully.
   a Why   b When   c Who

4 _____ saw the accident?
   We did.
   a Where   b Who   c Why

5 _____ did it happen?
   It was early in the morning!
   a Why   b Where   c When

Unit 10

Answer the quiz show questions. Circle *a*, *b* or *c*.

0   Is Madrid the capital of Spain?
  a Yes they are.
  (b) Yes, it is.
  c Yes, it will.

1   Did the Chinese invent writing?
  a Yes, they did.
  b No, they won't.
  c Yes, they could.

2   Is the River Nile in South America?
  a Yes, they did.
  b No, it won't.
  c No, it isn't.

3   Will the next Olympics Games be in London?
  a No, he didn't.
  b No, they won't.
  c No, they can't.

4   Is the Atlantic the biggest ocean?
  a No, it isn't.
  b Yes, it could.
  c No, it won't.

5   Were the Pyramids built by the Spanish?
  a No, he couldn't.
  b No, they weren't.
  c No, it wasn't.

6   Are kangaroos Chinese?
  a Yes, it is.
  b No, they don't.
  c No, they aren't.

7   Could the Romans speak English?
  a Yes, they could.
  b No, they weren't.
  c No, they didn't.

8   Was Shakespeare German?
  a No, he wasn't.
  b No, he didn't.
  c No, he couldn't.

9   Can penguins fly?
  a No, they can't.
  b No, they couldn't
  c No, they won't.

10 Have computers changed our lives?
  a Yes, they do.
  b Yes, they did.
  c Yes, they have.

11 Is the River Thames in England?
  a Yes, it does.
  b Yes, it will.
  c Yes, it is.

12 Was the U.S. an English colony?
  a Yes, it was.
  b Yes, it does.
  c Yes, it could.

Exam Time

Unit 11

A Read the sentences about the Earth.
Circle the best words (*a*, *b*, or *c*) for each space.

0 Mountains _____ by movements deep inside in the Earth.
   (a) are made   b is made   c make

1 Clouds _____ when the water drops cool.
   a forms   b are formed   c forming

2 When sunlight _____, you can see a rainbow.
   a colors   b will split   c is split

3 Steam _____ when water is boiled.
   a is made   b makes   c made

4 Electricity _____ on the wind farm using turbines or windmills.
   a heats   b is generated   c generates

5 When gases _____, you can make fire.
   a have burned   b are burned   c will burn

6 Lightning _____ by a thunderstorm.
   a is produced   b has produced   c produced

B There's a volcano and it's about to erupt! What happens?
Circle the best answer (*a*, *b* or *c*).

0 People are asked to leave …
   (a) by the police.   b by the mountain.   c by the volcano.

1 They collect their things and leave …
   a by the scientists.   b by bus.   c by their friends.

2 Some people are rescued …
   a by the mountain.   b by helicopter.   c by their houses.

3 The noise of the volcano is heard …
   a by stereo.   b by the mountain.   c by people far away.

4 Rocks and lava are collected for experiments …
   a by the police.   b by the scientists.   c by the tourists.

5 The villagers' crops are covered …
   a by the ash.   b by the scientists.   c by the volcano.

6 Crops are grown on volcanic land …
   a by scientists.   b by farmers.   c by tourists.

Unit 12

A Read the article about building a theme park.
Write the best words (*a*, *b* or *c*) for each space.

The theme park ⁰ __a__ very quickly and the project took only two years to complete. It ¹ _____ to be an adventure park, suitable for the whole family. There were shops and cafés all around the park, and places to sit by the river.

The park ² _____ in 2012 by the mayor. One year later, two hotels ³ _____ inside the grounds and a new train station ⁴ _____ nearby.

The theme park was popular with local people and companies, and it ⁵ _____ the Best New Business Award that year.

0	a was built	b	build	c	is built
1	a designed	b	was designed	c	is designing
2	a is opening	b	open	c	was opened
3	a were built	b	was built	c	are built
4	a is constructed	b	were constructed	c	was constructed
5	a was given	b	is given	c	gave

B Read the sentences. Circle *a* or *b*.

1 The park _____ in 2012.
   a was opened *(circled)*
   b is opened

2 The adventure activities _____ for children and adults.
   a was designed
   b were designed

3 A café _____ near the entrance.
   a was constructed
   b is constructed

4 One year later, a new train station _____ nearby.
   a was built
   b were built

5 Last year, the park _____ an award for safety.
   a is given
   b was given

Unit 13

A Read the sentences about Alex's birthday. What is the missing adverb of frequency? The first letter is already there. There is one space for each letter in the word.

0 I don't o f t e n go to bed after nine o'clock, but I did today!
1 I u _ _ _ _ _ _ have a party with my friends.
2 S _ _ _ _ _ _ _ _ _ we go into town together, and other times we go to my house.
3 My parents a _ _ _ _ _ buy me a present.
4 But they n _ _ _ _ give it to me in the morning. I have to wait until the evening dinner!

B Read the story about Nasruddin. Write the best word (*a*, *b* or *c*) for each space.

It was a ⁰ _b_ day. Nasruddin went to the palace to have dinner with the king. He was very ¹ _____. The food looked ² _____! There was so much to eat: tender chicken with rice, tasty meat stews, ³ _____ salads, sweet fruit, and ⁴ _____ desserts.

Nasruddin sat down to eat. The king asked Nasruddin about the meat stew. "What do you think? Do you like it?"

"Oh yes, I do. It's ⁵ _____!"

"Really? Do you think so?" said the king. "I don't agree. I think it's a very ⁶ _____ stew."

"Yes, your majesty," said Nasruddin, "You are right. It isn't ⁷ _____ at all."

"What?" said the king. "I don't understand. You just told me that the stew was ⁸ _____."

"I did say that," answered Nasruddin, "but I serve the king, not the stew."

0 **a** high	**b** sunny	**c** friendly
1 **a** busy	**b** sad	**c** happy
2 **a** delicious	**b** pretty	**c** kindly
3 **a** fresh	**b** hard	**c** old
4 **a** nicely	**b** terrible	**c** wonderful
5 **a** awful	**b** fantastic	**c** quietly
6 **a** bad	**b** good	**c** noisy
7 **a** good	**b** badly	**c** bad
8 **a** interesting	**b** fantastic	**c** cold

C Complete the five conversations. Circle *a*, *b* or *c*.

0   I think it's broken.
    a   I'll ask her politely.
    (b) Don't worry—I'll open it carefully.
    c   Yes, I'm late.

1   Can you hurry?
    a   Yes, I'll come quickly.
    b   Yes, I'll come slowly.
    c   It's noisy.

2   Please work quietly.
    a   Yes, OK.
    b   I hope so.
    c   Not at all.

3   Give me the fruit!
    a   Please walk carefully.
    b   Please ask politely.
    c   Please eat silently.

4   Open your present carefully.
    a   Yes, I'm here.
    b   It's usually closed.
    c   Yes, I will.

5   Don't run fast in here.
    a   Maybe. It's late.
    b   No, I'll run quickly.
    c   OK, I'll walk slowly.

Unit 14

Complete the conversation. What do the children say at their school board meeting? Write the correct letter (*a–h*).

Jeremy   How can we make our school "greener", Rachel?
Rachel   0 _h_
Jeremy   Perhaps if we talked about it at the school board meeting, we'd get some ideas.
Rachel   1 ___
Jeremy   Let's go and talk to them now. What do you think about solar energy?
Matt   2 ___
Jeremy   I agree. How else could we save the school some money?
Isabel   3 ___
Jeremy   That's a great idea. We could put notes next to the light switches to help us remember.
Rachel   4 ___
Jeremy   Yes. We should do that. And the printers, too.
Rachel   5 ___
Jeremy   OK. We can ask the teachers about it tomorrow.

a   Yes, I think you're right.
b   If we asked the teachers to do it, too, we'd save even more.
c   It's important. If the school fitted solar panels to the roof, we would save money.
d   Yes, I'd like to walk to school.
e   If we always turned off the lights, we'd save electricity and money.
f   Me, too.
g   If we turned off the computers too, that would help.
h   I'm not sure.

Unit 15

Read Kirsty's blog about her trip to visit her penfriend Marie, who lives in Australia. Are the sentences right (circle *a*) or wrong (circle *b*)? If there is not enough information to answer right or wrong, choose *Doesn't say* (circle *c*).

We set off early in the morning to the airport. It was still dark and I felt tired. My parents told me not to worry, but I felt nervous before I got on the plane. It was such a long trip. I felt cold on the plane and the flight attendant gave me a blanket. Eventually, I arrived in Australia. Everyone sounded strange to me. I've never heard people speak English before! The shops and houses looked different, too. When I arrived at Marie's house, I felt happy. My room looked really pretty, and there were nice pictures on the walls. Marie's mom cooked dinner, and it smelled fantastic. She's a great cook. The food tasted different to my mom's, but I liked it. I called home and told my parents that I would be OK.

0 Kirsty lives in Australia.
   a Right   (b) Wrong   c Doesn't say

1 Kirsty traveled to Australia by plane.
   a Right   b Wrong   c Doesn't say

2 She felt happy before the trip.
   a Right   b Wrong   c Doesn't say

3 She felt hungry on the flight.
   a Right   b Wrong   c Doesn't say

4 People's accents sounded strange to Kirsty.
   a Right   b Wrong   c Doesn't say

5 The shops looked the same as shops in her country.
   a Right   b Wrong   c Doesn't say

6 Kirsty liked the way the food tasted.
   a Right   b Wrong   c Doesn't say

Unit 16

Which notice (*a–h*) says this (1–5)?

0 It's dangerous to sit here.
1 It's possible to learn circus skills here after class.
2 It's impossible to get a ticket for the performance.
3 It's easy to get a drink here.
4 It's easy to find information.
5 It's safe to park here.

a Circus Show now closed. Sold out!
b Concert performers only.
c Circus programme available in all languages.
d Theatre café open all day.
e Car park open. Attendant on duty 24 hours.
f No seating. Risk of fire.
g Emergency exit this way.
h School circus club now open every evening!

Unit 17

You live in a new house near a castle. Write a note to tell your friend about the castle.

Say:
- What the castle is called and who comes to see it.
- When it is a good time to visit.

Write 25–35 words.

Unit 18

A Complete the sentences about life in a castle. Write the best word (*a*, *b* or *c*).

0 The queen __a__ coming to the banquet tonight.
   a is   b are   c will

1 We _____ prepared many different dishes.
   a will   b were   c have

2 They are going to _____ the prince's wedding.
   a celebrate   b celebrates   c celebrated

3 The cook said that the queen _____ planning to arrive by sunset.
   a was   b has   c be

4 He _____ worked hard all day.
   a is   b was   c has

5 We _____ be able to watch the banquet.
   a aren't   b don't   c won't

6 I _____ the bread.
   a makes   b making   c made

7 I _____ looking forward to the banquet.
   a will   b am   c do

8 I hope the queen _____ like the food we have cooked.
   a will   b is   c has

B Complete the conversation. Write *a* or *b*.

1 Let's go to the park. There's _____ children's festival today.
   a – (no article)   b a

2 I saw a poster. It's _____ interesting festival.
   a a   b an

3 I'm not sure. I don't usually like _____ festivals.
   a – (no article)   b a

4 You'll love it! And we can go on _____ fairground rides. They are amazing!
   a a   b the

5 OK. Let's call our _____ friends and ask them to come, too.
   a the   b – (no article)

Grammar Reference

Present Perfect

Use the present perfect to talk about things you've done in your life up to now.
I *have read many books about animals.*

Use short answers to questions in the present perfect to avoid repetition.
Have you fed the lions?
Yes, I have. / No, I have not.

Present Perfect Continuous

Use the present perfect continuous to talk about an action that started in the past and is continuing now.
I have been working here for twenty years.
We have been helping to protect endangered species. (We are still protecting them now.)
Have you been working with animals a long time?
Yes, I have. / No, I have not.

Use *for* to talk about a period of time.
I've been working at the zoo for three years.
Use *since* to talk about a moment in the past.
I have been brushing the ponies since 7:00 pm.

Future with *Will* / *Will Not* and *Going To*

Use *will / will not* to talk about facts in the future.
The "Copterbike" will work as a motorbike and will travel at 200 miles an hour.
You will not need to wear a helmet.

Use *will / will not* to make predictions about things you believe.
There will be fewer accidents.

Use *going to* to talk about future plans.
In our next program, we are going to look at a new invention.

Use *going to* to make predictions about things you see.
I think you can see that I am going to have lots of fun!

Future with Present Continuous

Use the present continuous to talk about future plans, especially when you mention a specific time or place.
Next week after school, Sultan and I are meeting to design our model spaceship.
We are building the real model in June.

Reported Speech with *Said That*

Use reported speech to tell someone what another person said.

Direct Speech	Reported Speech
I am in a cave.	He said that he was in a cave.
We are getting cold.	They said that they were getting cold.
I cannot walk.	He said he could not walk.

Reported Speech with *Told* and *Asked*

Use *said* in reported speech if you don't say who the person was talking to.

"Ants live in giant nests."   The guide *said* that ants lived in giant nests.

Use *told* in reported speech when you say who the person was talking to.

Use a name or object pronoun.

The guide *told me* that ants lived in giant nests.

Reported Questions

For reported questions, use *asked* + name or object pronoun + *if* or *whether*.

"Do ants eat flowers?"   Farid asked *her if / whether* ants ate flowers.

For reported questions with question words, change the word order back to a normal affirmative sentence.

"Where are the ants?"   I asked her *where* the ants *were*.

Simple Present Passive

We can say the same things in two different ways by using active or passive sentences.

The ash buries the crops. (active)   The crops *are buried by the ash*. (passive)

We often put the most important information at the start of the sentence.

In the first sentence, the focus is on the ash. In the second sentence, the focus is on the crops.
We make the simple present passive with subject + *am / is / are* + past participle (*seen*, *played*, etc).

Simple Past Passive

We make the simple past passive with subject + *was / were* + past participle (*seen*, *played*, etc.)
The village *was opened*.

Unreal Conditional

Use the unreal conditional to talk about something that probably will not happen.

If we *turned off* the lights, we *would save* electricity. (But we do not turn off the lights.)

Infinitive as Subject

Use *it is* + adjective + infinitive to give your opinions or to say what you think.

It is nice to meet you.   *It is easy to learn* how to juggle, but *it is difficult to do* it well!
They speak so quickly, *it is impossible to understand* them!

Grammar Reference

Irregular Verbs

Base Form	Past simple	Past participle
be	was / were	been
become	became	become
break	broke	broken
bring	brought	brought
build	built	built
bury	buried	buried
buy	bought	bought
catch	caught	caught
choose	chose	chosen
come	came	come
cost	cost	cost
cut	cut	cut
do	did	done
drink	drank	drunk
drive	drove	driven
eat	ate	eaten
feed	fed	fed
feel	felt	felt
find	found	found
fly	flew	flown
get	got	gotten
give	gave	given
go	went	gone
grow	grew	grown
have	had	had
hear	heard	heard
hide	hid	hidden
hit	hit	hit
hold	held	held
hurt	hurt	hurt
keep	kept	kept
know	knew	known
leave	left	left
lie	lay	lain

Base Form	Past simple	Past participle
light	lit	lit
lose	lost	lost
make	made	made
meet	met	met
pay	paid	paid
put	put	put
read	read	read
ride	rode	ridden
ring	rang	rung
run	ran	run
say	said	said
see	saw	seen
sell	sold	sold
send	sent	sent
show	showed	shown
sing	sang	sung
sink	sank	sunk
sit	sat	sat
sleep	slept	slept
speak	spoke	spoken
spend	spent	spent
steal	stole	stolen
stick	stuck	stuck
swim	swam	swum
take	took	taken
teach	taught	taught
tell	told	told
think	thought	thought
throw	threw	thrown
understand	understood	understood
wake up	woke up	woken up
wear	wore	worn
win	won	won
write	wrote	written